CHASING ADULTHOOD

An Interactive Character Study Guide
for Christian Tweens and Their Families

written by
Teri Friesen

Illustrated by
Deborah Smith

You will seek me and find me when you seek me with all your heart.
Jeremiah 29:13

Chasing Adulthood @ 2022 Teri Friesen

All rights reserved. No part of this publication may be reproduced or transmitted in any form or by any electronic or mechanical means including photo copying, recording, or any information storage and retrieval system now known or to be invented, without permission in writing from the publisher or the author.

Name: Friesen, Teri
Title: *Chasing Adulthood* by Teri Friesen
Illustrations: Deborah Smith
Cover design and graphics: Robert Ousnamer
Identifiers: LCCN: 2022915821
ISBN: 978-1-953114-71-6
Subjects: 1. Education: Homeschooling
2. Family and Relationships: Parenting/General

*All scripture verses referenced are from the NIV translation unless otherwise noted

About the Author photo by Selena Frey, From: Have and To Hold Photography haveandtoholdphotography@gmail.com used with permission.

Published by
EABooks Publishing
Your Partner In Publishing
a division of
Living Parables of Central Florida, Inc. a 501c3

EABooksPublishing.com

Dedication

This book is dedicated to my children, Hannah, Mitchell, and Alex, strong young men and women of God. Thank you for being my inspiration for writing this curriculum. You all have taught me so much about being a mom and how to love you as individuals, appreciating your unique strengths and weaknesses. I did not mother perfectly, but I thank you for your patience and grace as I attempted to parent the best way I could, guided by the perfect parent: JESUS!

I hope the truths you learned through your own journeys into godly adulthood will hold you fast as you navigate life with its ups and downs, joys and sorrows. I pray that one day, if the Lord blesses you with sweet children of your own, you will use this book as a guide in training them to chase after God with reckless abandon. I love you with my whole heart!

Mom

About the Author

Teri and her husband, Steve, have three children and live in Lakewood, Colorado. She enjoys writing, reading, caring for her flowerpots, meeting friends for coffee, participating in Bible study and leading worship at her church. Shortly after she and Steve were married, they moved to the Bay Area of Northern California where they lived for twenty-five years and raised their family. The Lord clearly called them to Colorado in 2019 and they have never looked back! They consider this home and feel very blessed to live a much more stress-free life. They appreciate the wide-open spaces, beautiful mountains, and their caring and connected neighborhood.

When daughter Hannah was about to enter elementary school, they decided to homeschool as it provided the ability to teach their kids at their own pace. They also desired to give them a broad knowledge base of learning as their children were ready to receive it. When Hannah entered her teen years, they looked for a thorough character trait study that would not only provide excellent Bible knowledge but a personal, practical application that would set her, and their other children, on the road to a lifetime of godly character. Not pleased with the available options, Teri decided to create her own curriculum which became their Bible class for that year. Two years later when their oldest son, Mitchell, was getting ready to launch into his teens, they did the same for him, tweaking the program to suit his needs and personality. Now, with one graduated and married and the other almost through college, both kids speak highly of the knowledge they gained through the intensive study and recall with fondness the lessons they learned. Teri and Steve's youngest middle school aged son, Alex, has just begun to walk through the Chasing Adulthood study. With some learning challenges, moderate ADHD, and anxiety, the program looks differently for him. It was important to Teri, as she wrote these materials, to consider families with children with alternative learning needs. The curriculum needed to be just as effective and impactful, yet not overwhelming to these children. A separate section after each chapter is dedicated to these unique families.

Teri has a deep desire to see families raise godly children who not only know and understand the Bible, but live it out in their everyday lives, seeking Christ above all things. Equipping parents to do just that is her passion and joy.

Table of Contents

PART ONE
About the Book – For Parents and Students

1.	What is *Chasing Adulthood*?	1
2.	Exploring the Book	2
3.	How is This Different from Other Character Education Studies?	2
4.	Benefits of This Program for Parents	4

PART TWO
Character Trait Studies – For Students

1	Servanthood vs. Self-Centeredness	9
	Monthly Planning Sheet	10
	Service Project Pages	11
	Godly Trait Description	17
	Scripture Study	17
	Biblical Figure Study	17
	Pitfall Description	18
	Scripture Study	18
	Biblical Figure Study	19
	Homework Questions	20
	Girls and Guys Only Questions	21
	Historical Figure Study	25
	Media Option	27
	Mentoring	27
	Journal Page	28
	Alternative Learning Pages	29
2	Sexual Purity vs. Sexual Immorality	35
	Monthly Planning Sheet	36
	Godly Trait Description	37
	Scripture Study	37
	Biblical Figure Study	38
	Pitfall Description	38
	Scripture Study	38
	Biblical Figure Study	39
	Homework Questions	40
	Girls and Guys Only Questions	42
	Historical Figure Study	48
	Media Option	50
	Mentoring	50
	Journal Page	51

	Purity Ring Discussion Pages	52
	Alternative Learning Pages	54
3	Discipline vs. Laziness	57
	Monthly Planning Sheet	58
	Godly Trait Description	59
	Scripture Study	59
	Biblical Figure Study	60
	Pitfall Description	61
	Scripture Study	61
	Biblical Figure Study	61
	Homework Questions	62
	Girls and Guys Only Questions	63
	Historical Figure Study	66
	Media Option	68
	Mentoring	68
	Journal Page	69
	Alternative Learning Pages	70
4	Compassion vs. Indifference	75
	Monthly Planning Sheet	76
	Godly Trait Description	77
	Scripture Study	77
	Biblical Figure Study	77
	Pitfall Description	78
	Scripture Study	78
	Biblical Figure Study	79
	Homework Questions	80
	Girls and Guys Only Questions	81
	Historical Figure Study	84
	Media Option	85
	Mentoring	85
	Journal Page	86
	Alternative Learning Pages	87
5	Integrity vs. Dishonor	91
	Monthly Planning Sheet	92
	Godly Trait Description	93
	Scripture Study	93
	Biblical Figure Study	93
	Pitfall Description	94
	Scripture Study	94
	Biblical Figure Study	94
	Homework Questions	95
	Girls and Guys Only Questions	97

	Historical Figure Study	100
	Media Option	102
	Mentoring	102
	Journal Page	103
	Alternative Learning Pages	104
6	**Courage vs. Cowardice**	107
	Monthly Planning Sheet	108
	Godly Trait Description	109
	Scripture Study	109
	Biblical Figure Study	110
	Pitfall Description	110
	Scripture Study	110
	Biblical Figure Study	111
	Homework Questions	112
	Girls and Guys Only Questions	113
	Historical Figure Study	116
	Media Option	118
	Mentoring	118
	Journal Page	119
	Alternative Learning Pages	120
7	**Self-Control vs. Self-Indulgence**	125
	Monthly Planning Sheet	126
	Godly Trait Description	127
	Scripture Study	127
	Biblical Figure Study	128
	Pitfall Description	128
	Scripture Study	129
	Biblical Figure Study	129
	Homework Questions	131
	Girls and Guys Only Questions	133
	Historical Figure Study	136
	Media Option	137
	Mentoring	137
	Journal Page	138
	Alternative Learning Pages	139
8	**Humility vs. Pride**	143
	Monthly Planning Sheet	144
	Godly Trait Description	145
	Scripture Study	145
	Biblical Figure Study	146
	Pitfall Description	146
	Scripture Study	147

	Biblical Figure Study	147
	Homework Questions	149
	Girls and Guys Only Questions	150
	Historical Figure Study	153
	Media Option	155
	Mentoring	155
	Journal Page	156
	Alternative Learning Pages	157
9	Obedience vs. Disobedience	161
	Monthly Planning Sheet	162
	Godly Trait Description	163
	Scripture Study	163
	Biblical Figure Study	164
	Pitfall Description	164
	Scripture Study	165
	Biblical Figure Study	165
	Homework Questions	166
	Girls and Guys Only Questions	168
	Historical Figure Study	171
	Media Option	173
	Mentoring	173
	Journal Page	174
	Alternative Learning Pages	175
10	Wisdom vs. Foolishness	179
	Monthly Planning Sheet	180
	Godly Trait Description	181
	Scripture Study	181
	Biblical Figure Study	182
	Pitfall Description	182
	Scripture Study	182
	Biblical Figure Study	183
	Homework Questions	184
	Girls and Guys Only Questions	186
	Historical Figure Study	188
	Media Option	189
	Mentoring	189
	Journal Page	190
	Alternative Learning Pages	191
11	Forgiveness vs. Anger	195
	Monthly Planning Sheet	196
	Godly Trait Description	197
	Scripture Study	197

Biblical Figure Study	198
Pitfall Description	198
Scripture Study	199
Biblical Figure Study	199
Homework Questions	200
Girls and Guys Only Questions	202
Historical Figure Study	205
Media Option	206
Mentoring	206
Journal Page	207
Alternative Learning Pages	208

PART THREE
Ceremony and Celebrations – For Parents and Students

1. Informal Celebration Options	211
2. Formal Celebration Options	213
A. Type of Formal Celebrations	213
B. Formal Ceremony Components	214
C. Celebration Planning Pages	216
Certificate of Completion	219

PART FOUR
Resource guide – For Parents and Students

1. Lists	220
2. Additional Resources	223
3. Templates	226
4. FAQs	235

PART FIVE
Answer Keys – For Parents

Homework/Alternative Learning Activities Answer Key	240
Citations	254

PART ONE

1. What is *Chasing Adulthood*?

As Christian parents, our goal for our children is to train them up to be men and women who love God and others. We want them to serve out of a knowledge and understanding of who God made them to be. However, we may not know exactly how to do that. Today's young people are growing up with challenges that we never had. Society feeds them subtle lies that are hard to counteract. Our kids are bombarded with messages that are the opposite of what the Bible teaches. In a world where there is no absolutes and truth "is what you make it", we as parents often struggle to fight against the raging tide. We may read devotionals with them, pray, and even encourage their attendance in a church youth group. Some also attend Christian school. We all do our best to lead by example, but could there be more to how we prepare them to be godly adults? Is there something else we can do to intentionally infuse them with the strength of character they need to navigate life's twists and turns?

This curriculum will do just that! *Chasing Adulthood* serves as a guide to going deeper with your child. An intensive study in what it means to be godly, the program allows your child to dig into the Bible, learn various character traits, receive mentoring by respected adults, serve their community, and memorize Scripture. Homework, reading, and service projects layer the learning, making for a meaningful experience, thinking through real life applications. The completion of the program can be celebrated with an optional ceremony. This ceremony creates a moment in time, a beachhead, that can be remembered for a lifetime. Jewish families have done it well with a Bat or Bar Mitzvah when their children come of age. The Christian tradition has not made such a cornerstone of entering manhood or womanhood from a biblical perspective. The goal is to set a firm foundation of godly character and then launch our young people, with the blessing of the family, into the next stage of their spiritual journey.

The program can be used for any type of schooling environment (home school or traditional school) as well as for special needs children. The homeschooled child may have the time to finish each section of every chapter. The traditionally schooled child can work through the sections that fit best with their schedule and simply leave the other areas blank. For special needs children, every chapter has its own section of pages adapted to fit different learning modalities and abilities. These families can use the chapter pages as is or use the adapted version depending on their child's specific needs.

The design of the book, with a chapter for each character trait, is set up for a month-long in-depth study of each trait. Broken down into weekly segments, the format works well as a nine-month study, or a school year-long study. If you find that to be too much time, you could truncate the assignments and work through two traits in one month. The longer you can spend on this the better, as it provides an opportunity for in-depth study and focus. But even a few months will produce an excellent Scripture base and understanding from which to launch your son or daughter. If you feel you cannot commit to a minimum of four months, it would be best to find another curriculum that better suits your needs.

My hope is that this program will inspire you to go deeper with your child, teaching them what it means to be a man or woman of God, giving them the tools to step into the world with courage and strength of character.

Thank you for investing in the spiritual life of your children and using Chasing Adulthood as your tool. May the Lord richly bless your family as you strive to know him better.

2. Exploring the Book

There are several sections to this workbook. Part One is an explanation of how to use the material.

Part Two is the meat of the book where the student will dive into Scripture and learn all about godly character and pitfalls. Each chapter has several homework components they can work through page by page or selectively based on time commitments. If you have multiple students completing the workbook at the same time, or you want to do the program with younger siblings when they come of age, it is recommended that you make copies of the student pages, so you always have the original book as your master copy, purchasing only one book. You may, instead, choose to have the book spiral bound, a few dollars at a copy store, for each student to have their own.

Part Three focuses on the celebratory ceremony. Some folks may opt out of this all together. Though certainly optional, it is highly encouraged to do some sort of celebration after completing this rigorous study. Since it is an individual choice to have a ceremony and to also choose what type you are comfortable with, this section is full of ideas of how to celebrate in all sorts of ways: formal, informal, big, small, etc. Planning pages are included for you to record your ideas, timelines, guest list, and so on. Guided questions will help you walk through how to prepare, setting you up for the right type of ceremony for you and your child.

Part Four is your resource guide. Included here are several lists of additional scriptures, traits and pitfalls, biblical characters, and historical characters for reference. Additional resources are provided for further study and to direct you to other material that may assist you in your journey. Also in this section are templates if you choose to add to the program with your own selected traits. We highly encourage you to customize this program for your child. If you do not see something you want your child to study, use the templates provided to customize their individualized program. Finally, a FAQ section is provided to answer any questions you might have as you go through the book. I encourage you to read through the FAQs before starting, as they may provide direction and insight into how best to approach the study.

Lastly, Part Five contains the homework answer keys for both the homework sections of each trait as well as the alternative learning section of each chapter.

3. How is this program different than other character education studies?

We recognize there are many great studies, devotionals, and curriculums that have taught character traits. Do we really need another one? What makes *Chasing Adulthood* so different?

Four components make this a unique study experience: content, mentoring, service projects, and celebration ceremony.

The first component is *content*, or what is being studied. This is more than a study in godly character. Godly traits are examined, but so are the pitfalls to godliness. Knowing the pitfalls and what Scripture says about them is just as important as learning the godly traits. A study of biblical characters such as David, Joseph, and Esther, teaches our kids about courage, faith, and obedience. On the other hand, studying Peter, Jonah, and Potiphar's wife show how cowardice, disobedience, and lust hinder a relationship with God. There is also an opportunity to read about historical figures, past and present, who did positive things in the world due to the character traits they possessed. Studying a variety of people gives a broader understanding.

Several mediums are used in delivering the character trait content.

- *Homework* pages are provided for each character quality. The child dives into Scripture and studies characters who both honored God and displeased God with their choices. Real world examples and scenarios are explored to allow for life application. Homework is meaningful and applicable to what kids are facing today. After each general homework section there are a few short questions geared toward guys and girls separately. Godly character shows up differently in men and woman sometimes. A specific focus for each helps to bring it home.
- *Scripture study* and *memorization* help your child have a deeper understanding of the trait they are learning and what the Bible says about both traits and pitfalls.
- *Historical figures* study is an additional layer of learning. Reading about other figures in history and how they lived out these qualities helps provide greater application for our kids who need more than just the study of Bible characters.
- *Biographies or autobiographies* can also be part of the homework process. Students can choose to read a biography of their historical figure of choice and summarize in a report or synopsis. How that is done, whether a standard report or a more creative outlet, is up to your child.
- *Media* of various types related to the biblical or historical person referenced is a great way to solidify their knowledge and understanding, especially if your child is a visual or auditory learner.

By reading (Scripture and books), writing (homework pages and book reports), and observing (documentaries and movies), you are providing your child with an excellent foundation of knowledge, while utilizing different learning modalities.

The second component, and possibly the most important to the program, is *mentoring*. Please do *not* skip this step. Parents and students will identify Christian leaders, fellow parents, church staff, ministry leaders, or friends whom the child respects. These mentors work with your child during their study of character and teach by example what it means to live a life of discipline, humility, courage, or whatever traits you have chosen for your child to study. Examples of their mentor's struggles with their own pitfalls make for meaningful interactions. Some mentoring sessions may be a one-time meeting while others could last the duration of the program. Having other adults, who are not mom or dad, building into the lives of your children is a priceless gift they will always cherish. These positive role models can stay with your child for years to come and will be the people they turn to when life gets hard. Each trait has a mentoring component.

A *service project* is a third aspect that sets this curriculum apart from others. We do not simply want to provide a lot of head knowledge about the Bible without helping our kids turn that knowledge into action that serves others. Living out what they are learning helps solidify the character we want to see in our kids. Service opportunities can be a big project at the end of the study, or several smaller tasks completed throughout the study. Allow your child to make a list of places, organizations, or people they would like to serve, and find ways to make it happen! The service project is explained in the first character trait chapter of Servanthood.

A final component that makes this a unique study is the *celebration ceremony* upon completion. It is optional, of course, but could be a formal or informal event, recognizing the huge milestone of entering godly man or womanhood. Having a moment in time where your child is celebrated and honored for a job well done shows them the importance of what they have just accomplished. The idea of the ceremony is a marker that takes your son or daughter from childhood to godly man or womanhood. It is not intended to just be a fun party, but rather a ceremony of transition, a truly remarkable and life-changing experience. Whether big or small, take the time to commemorate this milestone.

4. Benefits of this program for parents

It is easy to give your child a workbook and have them complete the questions. While it is possible to learn and have a general understanding of character, the involvement of the parent(s) makes this study especially effective. Walking alongside your child reinforces the importance of what they are learning. It allows opportunity to share in their journey, see their understanding, hear their questions, interact with the material, and share your own journey of godly man or womanhood.

The mentoring portion of the program allows the parent to choose the influencers for their kids. Children are not going to do this for themselves. When mom and/or dad look at the godly people they know, they can make connections based on the character traits they will be teaching their kids.

Parental involvement does require time and effort. As mentioned above, it is easy to hand a workbook to our kids and have them fill in the blanks. A cornerstone purpose of this curriculum is intentionality. There is a specific purpose to what is in these pages. It takes your daughter or son from childhood to woman or manhood. It is a journey, a process. They should not walk it alone. Therefore, time and effort from mom and/or dad is required. Time commitments will vary based on your home situation, but you will short-change your child's learning if you simply hand off the book. It will not have the same effect or the same depth of meaning without your involvement and support.

As you walk through these pages you will be encouraged to see the learning that is taking place. Your kids will start to make connections as they study and memorize Scripture, compare the godly traits with the pitfalls, and apply that understanding to their own struggles. Working alongside provides many opportunities for conversation and generates discussion around topics such as morality, honesty, and faith. If you are there with them, you have made yourself available when the questions and confessions come up. You are opening the door for future honest conversations, long after the program is done. Creating a space where your kids feel safe sharing their heart is priceless and well worth the time it will take to go through the program with your child. You will not necessarily sit there as they do all the work, but a partner attitude is the most effective. Being involved each step of the way reinforces the importance of this curriculum to your kids. They are seeing you work hard to create service opportunities, mentoring relationships, and a celebration ceremony. It does make the process more meaningful to them.

Once you purchase this book you have access to the Chasing Adulthood Facebook member page. This page provides a space for sharing questions about the program as well as experiences of how God is using this book to bless your family. You can find us at www.facebook.com/groups/ChasingAdulthood.

PART TWO

CHARACTER STUDIES

Hey, kids, this is for you. In developing character, there are always godly and ungodly traits that can become part of our lives. Though we pray for the godly ways to take root, and that is the emphasis of this curriculum, it is important to also study what the pitfalls to godliness are, so we know what to guard against. When traveling down an unknown road, isn't it helpful for someone who has been where you are going to warn you about the pothole around the corner? Each character trait listed below has a godly trait and corresponding pitfall, several Scripture references addressing each, a biblical character that possesses that trait, either positively or negatively, homework pages, Bible memory, journaling pages, additional reading materials to layer your understanding, and mentoring ideas.

Every chapter starts with a monthly planning page. This is to help keep you organized and on track. Fill in the month you are studying that trait, which character trait you are studying, who your mentor will be for this trait, when you will meet, the Scripture verse you will memorize as well as which homework sections you will complete and on which weeks. You can break down each trait into manageable weekly steps so not to get overwhelmed with too much at once. A slow diligent pace will work well to provide the knowledge you are looking for. Consider the planning sheet as your organizer that you refer to each day, so you know what is next in your study. If you are a homeschooled student, you may be using this as a Bible curriculum. In this case, completing the program in its entirety is feasible and recommended. You can write on your planning sheet the sections you will do each week. Feel free to skip around if you do not like the order laid out in the book.

If you are a traditionally schooled student, your available time may be more limited. Before you begin a chapter look over each section and decide which portions you can complete and which sections you will skip. Do not skip the Scripture study or biblical figure studies as these are the bedrock of each chapter. You may find that one week you can add the historical figure section and another week you can include the media option. You can mark this down on your planning sheet. Each month may look different. I encourage you not to skip the same section each time but to alternate so you get to experience every section and enjoy the variety. If you find you have extra time you may enjoy filling in the section you missed.

For our students with alternative learning needs, or if you simply prefer less writing and more creative activities, there are several pages in the back of each chapter that are just for you. Depending on your abilities, you may decide to work through the original pages as they are, stick to only the adjusted pages in the back of each chapter, or do a mixture of both. A suggestion is to go over each section with mom or dad and decide if it is a section you would like to do. I encourage you to read the Scripture study and biblical character sections as the backdrop to the lesson. Then, jump to the alternative learning pages for activities related to those passages. If you feel up for the challenge, see if you can do some of the other sections of the chapter, such as the historical figure study or media option. The more you can complete, the deeper your understanding of that character trait will be. Use the planning sheet to keep you up to date on which sections you are working on and what is next.

We encourage each student using this book to keep a binder that they will use just for this study. Get some tab dividers and for each chapter studied, write the trait name on the divider. As you receive handouts or charts from your mentor, you can insert them into the appropriate chapter section. If you have made copies of the homework pages, when completed, you can insert them into the binder and refer to it as needed. Any alternative learning pages can be copied and inserted here as well. If you print off research or articles from the internet relating to a historical figure, or have additional notes or journal pages, these can be inserted into the chapter section of your binder. This will give you one place where you can access all the work you completed.

> Don't let anyone look down on you because you are young, but set an example for the believers in speech, in conduct, in love, in faith and in purity.
> 1 Timothy 4:12

Chapter One

Servanthood vs. Self-Centeredness

MONTHLY PLANNING PAGE

MONTH _____ CHARACTER TRAIT _____ PITFALL _____

HOMEWORK SECTION   **COMPLETED**   MENTOR _____
(insert on each line below the homework sections you will complete for this trait)

WEEK 1
_____   ☐ ☐ ☐ ☐   DATES WE MEET _____
_____
_____   MEMORY VERSE _____
_____
                                                                         HISTORICAL FIGURE _____
WEEK 2
_____   ☐ ☐ ☐ ☐   BIOGRAPHY/AUTOBIOGRAPGY TITLE (if applicable) _____
_____
_____   SEXUAL PURIITY STUDY GUIDE TITLE (if applicable) _____
_____

WEEK 3
_____   ☐ ☐ ☐ ☐   SERVICE PROJECTS (if applicable) _____
_____
_____   _____
_____
                                                                         DATES PROJECTS COMPLETED _____
WEEK 4
_____   ☐ ☐ ☐ ☐   _____
_____
_____   NOTES, PAPERS, RESEARCH INSERTED IN BINDER:
_____
                                                                         YES   NO

Service Project Explanation

The placement of servanthood first in the book is intentional. Since a project is associated with this trait, we want to give students the opportunity to choose several small projects to work on through the entirety of the curriculum study, or select one large project to do at the end of the program (or both if you chose). As you learn about the godly trait of servanthood and study how valuable it is, you will choose project(s) that reflect God's heart. These activities may be one day or repeat visits. We recommend doing one thing often or choosing multiple things to do throughout this program.

 **LOCAL OPPORTUNITIES**

- Serve at a homeless food kitchen
- Volunteer at an after-school program
- Babysit, free of charge, for a young family in your neighborhood or church
- Find other ways to serve your neighbors (lawn mowing, trash clean up – free of charge)
- Volunteer at church in a ministry that may outside your comfort zone
    - Ushering
    - Children's ministry
    - Nursery
    - Coffee cart
    - Maintenance
- Tutoring – free of charge
- Accompany your church groups on their community service days
- Read to children at your local library
- Volunteer at your local food bank
- Assemble care packages for health care workers or first responders
- Create a food drive at your school or church and distribute to your community
- Fundraise for a local need

 **NATIONAL or GLOBAL OPPORTUNITIES**

- Go on a mission trip and serve in another state or country
- Work at a special needs camp
- Sponsor a child and find ways to fundraise to support that child
- Contact a missionary in another part of the world and offer your time to support them locally

- Find an organization that does something you believe in and find ways to support their cause.
- Run a 5K or half marathon for World Vision to raise awareness and funds for clean water wells in Africa
- Research a third-world poverty issue and host an Awareness Party to share the plight.
- Incorporate a 24-hour fast or longer, while praying for the impoverished

Choose that type of service project you would like to do. You may be interested in multiple opportunities at your church, trying various areas of service spanning several months. When my son did this program, he opted to try various tasks at church such as working as a buddy in Sunday School, ushering, and leading elementary school worship. He also served lunches at an after-school program. He preferred the variety to one bigger project. Or you may work on a more international project doing some research and creating a single opportunity to serve. Another option is to take a mission trip for a more significant compacted experience at the end of your program or during summer break. My daughter went away for a week-long camp after her character study was complete. She worked for an organization that packed dried food packages that were sent all over the world to help feed the hungry. Depending on what you choose, there may be some planning required, so give yourself enough time to process and complete your project. Use the planning pages that follow to guide you.

Service Project Questionnaire

1. What type of project am I interested in (local or global)?

   _____

   If global, what are my options?

   _____

2. Who will I contact to start a conversation about joining this organization? (ministry representative, regional director, missionary, etc.)

   _____

   _____

   _____

3. What are my next steps in pursuing this opportunity?

   _____

   _____

   _____

   If local, do I want to serve in different capacities and provide a broad experience or focus in on one or two areas?

   _____

4. What are some areas of interest, based on the above ideas or some of my own?

   _____

   _____

   _____

5. Who do I contact to start a conversation about serving in this capacity? (pastor, youth director, organization leader, etc.)

6. What are my next steps in pursuing this opportunity?

Service Project Summary Page
Complete one page per project or opportunity

Fill out the top portion then at the conclusion of your service, fill out the summary questions.

Service Project:
_____

Service Dates:
_____

My responsibilities:

_____
_____
_____

My supervisor:

_____

Summary Questions:

1. Did I enjoy this area of service? Why or why not?

_____
_____
_____
_____

2. Was this out of my comfort zone?

_____

3. Would I enjoy this area of service on an on-going basis? Why or why not?

_____
_____

4. What did I learn about myself as I served? What was easy? What was hard?

_____

_____

_____

_____

5. How did the Lord stretch me and help me grow in this process?

_____

_____

_____

_____

Godly Trait – Servanthood

We serve out of a willing heart because Jesus was the ultimate servant. The goal is to practice being aware of the needs around me and acting with a willing spirit. Serving while complaining or with a begrudging attitude is not service as God intended.

"Prayer in action is love, and love in action is service. Try to give unconditionally whatever a person needs in the moment. The point is to do something, however small, and show you care through your actions by giving your time … We are all God's children, so it is important to share his gifts. Do not worry about why problems exist in the world – just respond to people's needs … We feel what we are doing is just a drop in the ocean, but that ocean would be less without that drop." - Mother Teresa [1]

Scripture Study

Deuteronomy 13:4
It is the LORD your God you must follow, and him you must revere. Keep his commands and obey him; serve him and hold fast to him.

Mark 10:45
For even the Son of Man did not come to be served, but to serve, and to give his life as a ransom for many.

Ephesians 6:7
Serve wholeheartedly, as if you were serving the Lord, not people.

Matthew 25:40
The King will reply, 'Truly I tell you, whatever you did for One of the least of these brothers and sisters of mine, you did for me.'

Biblical Figure Study

Tabitha (Dorcas) - Acts 9:36-42
In Joppa there was a disciple named Tabitha (in Greek her name is Dorcas); she was always doing good and helping the poor. About that time she became sick and died, and her body was washed and placed in an upstairs room. Lydda was near Joppa; so when the disciples heard that Peter was in Lydda, they sent two men to him and urged him, "Please come at once!" Peter went with them, and when he

arrived he was taken upstairs to the room. All the widows stood around him, crying and showing him the robes and other clothing that Dorcas had made while she was still with them. Peter sent them all out of the room; then he got down on his knees and prayed. Turning toward the dead woman, he said, "Tabitha, get up." She opened her eyes, and seeing Peter she sat up. He took her by the hand and helped her to her feet. Then he called for the believers, especially the widows, and presented her to them alive. This became known all over Joppa, and many people believed in the Lord. Peter stayed in Joppa for some time with a tanner named Simon.

Jesus – Read John 13:1-17

Jesus needed to teach his disciples how to serve. He showed them through his example that no one is above serving the other. Often service comes with humility. Think about that relationship as you read this story.

Pitfall – Self-Centeredness

Children are naturally self-centered. Life is all about them and getting their needs and wants met. The challenge is to redirect the focus to others. When you are constantly focused on self, you have an unbalanced view of the world around you. Your first thoughts are about your comfort or your structure rather than on what others around you may need.

 **Scripture Study**

Philippians 2:3-5
Do nothing out of selfish ambition or vain conceit. Rather, in humility value others above yourselves, not looking to your own interests but each of you to the interests of the others.

Psalm 119:36
Turn my heart toward your statutes and not toward selfish gain.

1 Corinthians 13:5
(Love) *It does not dishonor others, it is not self-seeking, it is not easily angered, it keeps no record of wrongs.*

Biblical Figure Study

<u>The Older Brother</u> – Luke 15-28-32
The older brother became angry and refused to go in. So, his father went out and pleaded with him. But he answered his father, 'Look! All these years I've been slaving for you and never disobeyed your orders. Yet you never gave me even a young goat so I could celebrate with my friends. But when this son of yours who has squandered your property with prostitutes comes home, you kill the fattened calf for him!'

"'My son,' the father said, 'you are always with me, and everything I have is yours. But we had to celebrate and be glad, because this brother of yours was dead and is alive again; he was lost and is found.'"

In the parable of the Lost Son, the younger son squanders his inheritance and upon losing everything returns home and begs his father for mercy. When the father celebrates the return of his son the older brother becomes angry and wonders when he would receive a party like his brother.

<u>Pharisees</u> – Matt. 23:1-3
Then Jesus said to the crowds and to his disciples: "The teachers of the law and the Pharisees sit in Moses' seat. So you must be careful to do everything they tell you. But do not do what they do, for they do not practice what they preach."

The Pharisees were always looking to protect themselves. Following God was based on rules and tradition rather than out of a heart of love for Him. They believed they were better than everyone else, stuck on self and their own personal righteousness.

Servanthood vs. Self-Centeredness Homework

1. Little is known of the biblical character Tabitha. This is the only reference to her in the Bible. What can we decipher about her from these verses?

2. Tabitha was an example of someone who saw a need in her own community and decided she could fill that need. Are you plugged into your local church or other organizations that make you aware of needs in the community in which you live? Have you served locally before? If so, list some of the ways you have served (within the church or your neighborhood).

3. In John 13, what was the significance of Jesus washing his disciples' feet? Why was this so hard for his disciples to witness and receive?

4. In the parable you read above in Luke 15, the older brother was jealous of his brother's welcome and showed selfishness in how he questioned his father. Do you think he was justified in his questions? Do you think it was selfishness that caused his anger?

5. Usually an overdose of "self" is what keeps us from wanting to serve others. List some of the reasons/excuses you can give for not serving.

6. Can you think of 3 ways you can serve your family, in your household?

7. Choose one of the verses of servanthood and commit it to memory. Reference the verse you chose here and record it on your monthly planning page.

Becoming a Woman of Service:

Hey gals, the following questions are just for you. Take the time to work through them, being as honest as you can.

The Bible is full of examples of service. From Jesus himself, to the disciples, to various women, we are taught the importance of serving, helping those in need, and showing Christ's kindness to those around us. Serving sometimes comes naturally for women because we are by nature more nurturing than our male counterparts. That is just how God made us. How does serving for women look differently than for men? Let's explore a few ideas.

1. If you are called to be a wife and mom, whether you also work outside the home or not, there are many built in ways you can serve your family. Depending on how husbands and wives and dads and moms have divided up household responsibilities, some tasks could be doing the grocery shopping, making the meals, paying the bills, taking out the garbage and mowing the lawn, to name a few. Can you think of other ways you could serve your family as an adult? Use the example of the adults you know personally.

2. Sometimes serving comes without thanks or appreciation. What can you do to keep an attitude of service especially when others do not acknowledge your efforts? Think about what your motivation should be in serving to help you answer this question.

3. Serving can get tiring. It is possible to serve too much and burn out because you have too many service obligations. Service can be fulfilling and sometimes it can be easy to take on too many things and say yes to too many requests. When that happens, you may become overwhelmed and start to lose track of what you are doing. Commitments break down and you become physically exhausted. It is just as important to understand your limits and to learn to say no to things as it is to serve others. Take a minute to think through all the ways you could possibly serve at your church. What might happen if you say yes to every need?

Serving families and our church and/or community is what Jesus is asking us to do. We show his love when we serve with an attitude of gratefulness. As a young woman who is choosing to develop godly character, think through where you could say yes more often and at the same time respecting your limits, so you do not burn out. If a candle is constantly burning, it will burn down too quickly, and the light goes out. Allow yourself the freedom to say no and rest.

Becoming a Man of Service:

Hey guys, the following questions are just for you. Take the time to work through them being as honest as you can. Let us chat about what serving looks like for you and how it is a part of godly manhood.

1. As you enter adulthood, all the things you have learned about servanthood as a young man will stick with you. If you have learned to serve your neighbors by cutting lawns or shoveling snow, chances are that will be a way you choose to serve when you are an adult. If you are used to serving in church now, then when you are an adult and have a family, continuing to serve in the church will be important to you. Good habits now will breed good habits later. What things would you want to teach your family about service? What lessons will you want them to learn?

2. How does a husband and father serve his family? You can list ways you see your own dad serving or maybe the example of a family friend or other adult male.

3. Being available to serve when the need arises is important. Learning to leave "white space" in your calendar means that you do not have every minute scheduled. It is a lot easier to serve when we are not rushing from event to event. If you learn to leave sections of time open, then it is easier to say yes when you become aware of a need. However, it is equally important to learn to say no. Knowing your limits helps you realize when you might not be the most effective. It is okay to say no to some things to avoid burning out. Why is learning the importance of rest necessary (not saying yes to everything)?

If you end up with a full-time job and are blessed to have a family as well, you may find it hard to serve. It can be tiring to juggle work and home life. Having extra jobs to do can add to a heavy load. It may take some practice to figure out how to include regular service opportunities into your busy schedule. God asks us all to serve, regardless of what our job or home situation is like. As you grow into adulthood you will learn the importance of balance. The priority is to have a willing heart and a desire to serve others. The Lord will help you figure out the rest.

Historical Figure

Choose a person from history (past or present) whom you feel exhibits qualities of servanthood. You may choose from the list provided in the resource guide in Part Four of this book or select one of your own. Do some research on this person (internet search, library books) and answer the following questions:

1. Why did you choose this individual?

2. What aspect of servanthood do they exhibit?

3. Explain how they lived this out in their daily life.

4. What obstacles, if any, did they have to overcome to serve in this way?

5. Complete the chart to identify their traits of servanthood vs. traits of self-centeredness.

Servanthood	Self-Centeredness

Biography/Autobiography

If you like to read, select a biography or autobiography on this individual to read throughout this month. Your parent may ask you to provide a book report or synopsis (personal choice for format) on what you read, paying special attention to their life of service.

 Media Option

Is there a movie or documentary on the historical figure you chose? If so, take some time to watch it and write down several things you can identify about their life of service.

 Mentoring

Choose a mentor who exhibits qualities of servanthood that you or your parent(s) admire. Maybe you know someone who has gone on several mission trips, volunteers weekly at a homeless shelter, regularly sacrifices financially to help others, or opens their home for those in need. Get together (how often is up to your parents/mentor, but often one meeting is sufficient as there are many other mentors involved in this process) and listen as they share their life experiences with you. Your parents will help guide the content of your discussions along with your mentor's ideas. If your mentor provides charts, lists, or diagrams as visuals, insert them into your binder for this chapter, along with any notes you may take. Possible discussion questions may include:
- I serve because…
- Sometimes serving is hard. Times when I did not serve because it was too hard were…
- Serving opportunities I've taken that I truly loved are…
- Serving opportunities I've taken that I did not like were…

Journal Page

1. What, if anything, did the Lord imprint on your heart during your study of servanthood?

2. What are your thoughts about the service project/projects you chose? If you have not yet completed your service project, do you feel this will be something easy for you to do or something that will require some sacrifice on your part?

3. If you have yet to complete your project(s), what do you hope to learn through the process of serving? Record your thoughts and feelings as you move through that process.

4. Spend some time in prayer talking to God about what you have learned, including the lessons you learned from your mentor.

5. Review your memory verse.

Alternative Learning Pages
Do all or some of the following 9 activities

Activity 1 - Read, or have someone read to you, the godly trait, pitfall, and corresponding Scripture verses at the beginning of this chapter. Do you understand the difference between servanthood and self-centeredness?

Activity 2 - Read, or have someone read to you, Acts 9:36-42. Fill in the first row of the chart below (or have someone fill it in for you).

	How did they serve?	Who did they serve?	Why did they serve?
Tabitha			
Jesus			

Read or have someone read to you John 13:1-17. Fill in the second row of the chart above (or have someone fill it in for you).

Activity 3 - Fill in the blanks with the appropriate word from the word bank based on the Bible passages above.

1. Tabitha made _____ for the people in her community.

2. _____ was the city where she lived.

3. _____ was the disciple who came and prayed over Tabitha when she died.

4. There were _____ gathered in the room where Tabitha died.

5. Before _____ Jesus ate in the upper room with the disciples.

6. During the meal Jesus _____ his disciples' feet.

7. The disciple Peter _____ what Jesus was doing.

8. The lesson Jesus was trying to teach his disciples was how to _____.

9. _____ would be considered self-centered.

10. The religious leaders believed they were more _____ than everyone else.

Robes	Cloaks	Righteous	Knowledge	Serve
Lydda	The Older Brother	John	Joppa	Peter
Widows	Pray	Passover	Paul	Questioned
Resurrection	Washed	Understood	Heated	Pharisees

Activity 4

1. What is the opposite of Servanthood?

_____

2. List 5 ways you can be self-centered.

_____

_____

_____

3. Describe a time you were selfish this week. What happened as a result? Write your answer or have someone write for you.

_____

_____

_____

_____

Activity 5 - Read, or have someone read for you, the following story. Answer the questions at the end.

Sharon and the Ice Cream Truck

Sharon, a 12-year-old red head, lived with her mom and dad in a small town in North Carolina. She loved riding her bike, catching frogs in the swamp behind her house, playing dress up with Madeline, her best friend, and reading adventure books. Sharon was excited because it was Thursday, and on Thursday the ice cream truck made its way down her long street. She would always swing on the little board swing tied up with ropes in her front yard, waiting for the faint sound of the jingle the truck would play as it slowly ambled up the road. With coins in her overalls pocket, she strained to see the truck on the dusty path. Thursday was her favorite day because there was not one thing she loved more than ice cream. Summers were so hot in North Carolina and often quite slow. She and her friends would always come running when they heard the truck, the most exciting thing to happen all week!

On this day, as Sharon stood on her swing peering down the road, her mom stepped onto the porch and called for her to come inside. She was not feeling well and was asking Sharon to please help with dinner. Sharon whined and complained because she had been waiting all week for her ice cream treat and had done a good job of not spending her money on other things. She asked if dad could help instead because she did not want to miss the ice cream truck. An argument ensued as Sharon insisted on having her way. However, she finally went inside, grumbling under her breath that she would have to wait another week before she could get her ice cream. She managed to help her mom with dinner but was frustrated and short tempered the rest of the night.

Before she went to bed, Sharon's mom sat with her and talked with her about what happened. She told Sharon that she had an opportunity to serve her by helping prepare dinner, but she missed out. Sharon was confused because she had helped her mom. The coins sitting in her pocket were proof that she had helped instead of going to the ice cream truck. Her mom explained that serving others is not simply a choice to do something for someone else, but rather the action must be accompanied by a willing heart for it to truly be an act of service. If the heart is focused on self, then it is not focused on serving someone else. Serving without a willing heart is empty. Sharon understood that she was being self-centered by demanding that she get her ice cream. She had been thinking of herself and what she was missing out on, even while she attempted to help her mom with dinner. She apologized for missing the point of servanthood and promised to do a better job of serving others when the opportunity arose.

1. Did Sharon serve her mom? Explain your answer.

_____

_____

2. What should have been Sharon's reaction to her mom to truly honor the Lord?

_____

_____

Activity 6 - Draw lines from the word Servanthood to other words that describe that trait.

Thoughtful

Funny   **Willing**

Sacrifice   **Kind**

Others   **Servanthood**   **Hard**

Myself   **Reject**

Take   **Give**

Frustrating

Activity 7 - If you like to draw, illustrate the above story from activity 5. When completed insert your drawing into your binder for this chapter.

Activity 8 - Fill in the blanks below with ways you can serve your family members and/or neighbors this month. Some ideas are listed for you but try to come up with your own.
    *Empty trash in the house
    *Take out garbage bins on garbage day
    *Make my sibling's bed for them without drawing attention to myself
    *Set the table every night before dinner without being asked
    *Do the dishes instead of walking away
    *Help my mom with the laundry
    *Clean up after our family pet
    *Mow the neighbor's lawn without payment
    *Walk the neighbor's dog
    *Help dad with yard work

1. One thing I can do each week to serve my mom is _____

2. I can serve my brother or sister each week by _____

3. When I am tempted to think about myself, I will first _____ before I do what I want.

4. When I see someone struggling to do a task I will _____ without being asked.

Activity 9 – Select one of the verses from the Scripture section of this study and put it to memory. If memorizing is hard, get creative. Put it to music, make it rhyme, write it out on notecards and repeat every morning.

Chapter Two

Sexual Purity vs. Sexual Immorality

MONTHLY PLANNING PAGE

MONTH _____ CHARACTER TRAIT _____ PITFALL _____

HOMEWORK SECTION   COMPLETED
(insert on each line below the homework sections you will complete for this trait)

WEEK 1
☐ ☐ ☐ ☐ MENTOR _____
_____
_____ DATES WE MEET _____
_____
_____

WEEK 2
☐ ☐ ☐ ☐ MEMORY VERSE _____
_____
_____ HISTORICAL FIGURE _____
_____ BIOGRAPHY/AUTOBIOGRAPGY TITLE (if applicable) _____
_____

WEEK 3
☐ ☐ ☐ ☐ SEXUAL PURITY STUDY GUIDE TITLE (if applicable) _____
_____
_____ SERVICE PROJECTS (if applicable) _____
_____
_____

WEEK 4
☐ ☐ ☐ ☐ DATES PROJECTS COMPLETED _____
_____
_____
_____ NOTES, PAPERS, RESEARCH INSERTED IN BINDER:
_____   YES   NO

Godly Trait – Sexual Purity

As Christian young people, God wants us to learn from an early age that he calls us to live a life of purity. Because we are set apart, we live set apart and choose to not give in to the culture that says anything we do with our bodies is okay.

In her book, *Reclaiming Intimacy*, Heather Jamison writes this about pre-marital sex, "Although peer support for virginity is sorely lacking, peer pressure to have sex comes in many forms. It appears outright as a challenge, or it surfaces in a confrontational way. It even comes clothed as a caring friend. For females, peer pressure is probably not as blatant, but it remains present. For males, sexual activity is often viewed as a trophy captured on one's way to manhood." [2]

PARENTS: An optional component in studying purity is presenting your child with a purity ring during their time of study. This can be a meaningful expression of reaffirming they belong to God. Reference the resource guide in Part Four of this book for purity ring resources. A discussion page to guide this process is at the end of this chapter. Sexual purity themes may include:
  Abstinence
  Your Body is a Temple
  Moral Purity

Scripture Study

1 Corinthians 6:19
Do you not know that your bodies are temples of the Holy Spirit, who is in you, whom you have received from God? You are not your own; you were bought at a price. Therefore, honor God with your bodies.

Matthew 15:19
For out of the heart come evil thoughts – murder, adultery, sexual immorality, theft, false testimony, slander.

1 Thessalonians 4:3
It is God's will that you should be sanctified: that you should avoid sexual immorality.

Hebrews 13:4
Marriage should be honored by all, and the marriage bed kept pure, for God will judge the adulterer and all the sexually immoral.

Psalm 139:13
For you created my inmost being; you knit me together in my mother's womb.

 # Biblical Figure Study

Joseph – Read Genesis 39

He was sold as a slave into the house of Potiphar of Egypt. Potiphar's wife found him to be attractive and tried to seduce him to go to bed with her. Joseph refused and ran off leaving his cloak behind. In anger Potiphar's wife accused him of sexual assault and he was thrown into prison. Joseph's refusal to sin and to stay pure despite the temptation was honored by God, even during personal grief and false accusations.

Pitfall – Sexual Immorality

Sexual immorality can be many things, impure thoughts, lust, and sex outside of marriage. These things dishonor God and are not how He intended for us to view our bodies or sex. A correct view of morality as Scripture describes it is necessary. Scripture is loud and clear how sexual immorality is not God's design. It cheats us of a fulfilling sexual experience with our future husband or wife and cheapens something that was created to be beautiful and satisfying. However, through God's grace there is a chance to reclaim what has been lost through forgiveness and repentance. There is no condemnation with Jesus and no need to live with shame and guilt. It is important to understand that grace is abundant, and nothing is beyond God's ability to forgive. And he does not hold grudges. Hope, grace, forgiveness, a fresh start. Thank you, Jesus!

 # Scripture Study

2 Corinthians 10:5
We demolish arguments and every pretension that sets itself up against the knowledge of God, and we take captive every thought to make it obedient to Christ.

1 Corinthians 6:13
You say, "Food for the stomach and the stomach for food, and God will destroy them both." The body, however, is not meant for sexual immorality but for the Lord, and the Lord for the body.

Ephesians 5:3
But among you there must not be even a hint of sexual immorality, or of any kind of impurity, or of greed, because these are improper for God's holy people.

Biblical Figure Study

<u>David</u> – Read 2 Samuel 11

Though he was considered a man after God's own heart, David struggled with sexual sin. He desired Bathsheba and rather than fleeing temptation he gave in and committed adultery. She got pregnant and, instead of coming clean and taking responsibility for his action, David had her husband, his good friend, murdered so they would not be found out. But God was not fooled and punished David greatly for his sin, deceit, and murder. Yet, he humbly approached God, confessed his moral failure and God went on to use him mightily. Our sin does not disqualify us in God's kingdom. Although, consequences may run deep God uses the good, bad, and ugly parts of our lives to accomplish his purposes. Praise God!

Sexual Purity vs. Sexual Immorality Homework - Part 1

1. Did Joseph's decision to flee temptation just happen or was this something he had determined in his heart, before confronted with the choice? Explain your answer.

2. Do our choices to remain sexually pure exempt us from persecution? Why or why not?

3. What can you do to flee temptation and not give in to sexual pressures (and this involves thought life, coarse joking, inappropriate physical contact, etc.)?

4. If you fall into sexual immorality, what does the Bible say about forgiveness and grace? About shame? Is it possible to renew your commitment to purity, moving forward with hope? Meditate on the following verses to provide insight to your answers.

Psalm 34:5
Those who look to him are radiant; their faces are never covered with shame.

Psalm 103:1-5, 8-12
Praise the LORD, my soul; all my inmost being, praise his holy name. Praise the LORD, O my soul, and forget not all his benefits – who forgives all your sins and heals all your diseases, who redeems your life from the pit and crowns you with love and compassion, who satisfies your desires with good things so that your youth is renewed like the eagle's. The Lord is compassionate and gracious, slow to anger, abounding in love, He will not always accuse, nor will he harbor his anger forever; he does not treat us as our sins deserve or repay us according to our iniquities. For as high as the heavens are above the earth, so great is his love for those who fear him, as far as the east is from the west, so far has he removed our transgressions from us.

Psalm 51:9
Hide your face from my sins and blot out my iniquity. Create in me a pure heart, O God, and renew a steadfast spirit within me. Do not cast me from your presence or take your Holy Spirit from me. Restore to me the joy of your salvation and grant me a wiling spirit, to sustain me.

Psalm 51:17
The sacrifices of God are a broken spirit; a broken and contrite heart, O God, you will not despise.

Hebrews 4:16
Let us then approach God's throne of grace with confidence, so that we may receive mercy and find grace to help us in our time of need.

PARENTS: This question is optional based on your child's maturity and readiness to discuss this controversial topic.

5. Today's culture fully embraces the LGBTQ+ lifestyle. What does the Bible teach about this subject? Identify 2-3 verses. Feel free to use the concordance section in the back of your Bible. Locate verses by theme or words. You can also do a google search for what the Bible says on certain topics to help you find key verses. Please note: not all websites are based on biblical information, so use caution when obtaining your information from the Internet.

6. What does the Bible teach about God's standard for loving people? Identify 2-3 verses.

7. Considering these truths, how do we as Christians respond to those who embrace this lifestyle?

_____

_____

_____

_____

It is important that as followers of Christ we refrain from taking a stand based on personal feelings, personal experience, or misinterpretation of Scripture. Our truth is formed ONLY from Scripture as God's Word. We also cannot pull one or two verses out of the Bible and make that a soap box, ignoring the entirety of the Bible and the character of God. **For further information and resources on this topic reference the resource guide in Part Four of this book.**

8. Choose one of the verses on sexual purity and commit it to memory. Reference the verse you chose here and record it on your monthly planning page.

_____

Becoming a Woman of Purity:

PARENTS: Your daughter may feel more comfortable going over these questions on her own or with the same sex parent. Honor her desire for privacy or to choose which parent she prefers. Or maybe she would prefer neither parent but choose to discuss with another trusted adult. The goal is for her to be honest so allow her to dig into these questions at her comfort level.

Hey gals, the following questions are just for you, and it is about to get real! This can be an uncomfortable topic. If you are not comfortable talking about sexual purity and similar topics, feel free to skip and come back when you or your parents feel you are ready.

As we learned from the trait description as well as the Scripture study, sexual immorality is not just about sex. It can be impure thoughts and lust as well as sex outside of marriage. Purity also involves modesty, how one dresses and presents their bodies to others. Purity can involve the kind of music we listen to. Do the words talk about casual sex, inappropriate or lewd behavior? All these areas speak to purity or impurity. "Finally, brothers and sisters, whatever is true, whatever is noble, whatever is right, whatever is pure, whatever is lovely, whatever is admirable—-if anything is excellent or praiseworthy—-think about such things" (Philippians 4:8).

Let's talk about modesty for a minute. Our culture today has an "anything goes" mentality. "It is my body, I can wear what I want" is a common response.

1. Why is it so easy for girls to be drawn into styles that are low cut, or high cut, tummy showing, short shorts and bras showing? What is the draw for you or for girls you know?

2. If you are a girl who does not feel comfortable dressing that way, have you experienced pressure from friends or other girls to give in? What does that feel like for you? Have you given in at times because it is hard to push against the pressure? *Yes* is a perfectly good answer because it is honest. Give yourself permission to explore your reasons.

3. If you are a girl who enjoys dressing this way, even periodically, think through the visual of what it might be like for boys who are trying to be pure in their thoughts. Let us be clear: It is *never* a girl's fault if a boy takes advantage of her because of how she dresses. We are all responsible for our own choices. However, consider this perspective. How does the biblical concept of "love your neighbor" come into play when thinking of the opposite sex and how you dress? Should there be a consideration of others when deciding what we wear? If you are unsure, ask yourself, are there times in Scripture when we are told to be considerate of others even if we feel we are not doing anything wrong? Look in the concordance in the back of your Bible or use an online concordance to help you find verses.

4. Try to project yourself twenty-five years down the road (I know, that's old!). You are a grown woman, possibly married. What lessons in purity will you want to have learned? Can your purity choices now affect your future relationships or a marriage?

Be encouraged! The Lord honors your desire for purity and will give you the strength you need to take a stand when others around you are making different choices. We want to view our bodies the way God sees us. That also means having a respectful view of others and their bodies. The young men you associate with will be someone's husband and father someday. Treat them with respect, treat yourself with respect, and honor one another. If you stumble into sin, there is always abundant grace and forgiveness. God is the God of second chances!

Becoming a Man of Purity:

PARENTS: Your son may feel more comfortable going over these questions on his own or with the same sex parent. Honor his desire for privacy or to choose which parent he prefers. Or maybe he would prefer neither parent but choose to discuss with another trusted adult. The goal is for him to be honest so allow him to dig into these questions at his comfort level.

Hey guys, the following questions are just for you. If you are not comfortable talking about sexual purity and similar topics, feel free to skip and come back when you or your parents feel you are ready.

As we learned from the trait description as well as the Scripture study, sexual purity is not just about sex. It can be purity in mind when watching inappropriate shows or movies, looking at magazines or pornography on the internet. Popular music often has impure messages kids listen to repeatedly. All these areas speak to purity or impurity. "Finally, brothers and sisters, whatever is true, whatever is noble, whatever is right, whatever is pure, whatever is lovely, whatever is admirable--if anything is excellent or praiseworthy--think about such things" (Philippians 4:8).

1. Guys are constantly being bombarded with visuals of girls not fully clothed or scantily clad women in movies, magazines, and social media. Our society is normalizing this kind of dress and often it is women who make guys feel guilty for even being attracted to what they see. What is your reaction when confronted with these types of images? How can you show respect for girls even when they dress immodestly? It is important to note here that regardless of how a girl dresses, boys are always responsible for their actions and behavior toward them. Immodesty is never an excuse to degrade or physically touch young ladies!

2. If you are a guy who has participated in crude joking or commented rudely to girls wearing certain kinds of clothing, just pause for a moment. Regardless of whether a young lady is dressed modestly or not, look at them through the eyes of Jesus. How does he see her? If she were your sister, would your initial reaction be different?

3. If you are a guy who works hard to be a young man of purity, what can you do to encourage your peers who may struggle to stand up for purity? What can you do to stand up for the purity of the young women in your life?

4. What does your thought life have to do with purity? Scripture says to "take captive every thought" (2 Cor. 10:5). Often what we think about we act on. Phil. 4:8 above gave a list of things to think about. Clearly what is in our minds is important to God. Is this an area of struggle for you? Sometimes it is hard to be honest, but there is incredible freedom in acknowledging our own areas of personal struggle.

5. Imagine yourself twenty-five years down the road (I know, that's old!). You are a grown man, possibly married. What lessons in purity will you hope to have learned? Can your purity choices now affect your future relationships or a marriage?

Be encouraged! The Lord honors your desire for purity and will give you the strength you need to take a stand when others around you are making different choices. We want to view our bodies the way God sees us. That also means having a respectful view of others and their bodies. The young women you associate with will be someone's wife and mother someday. Treat them with respect, treat yourself with respect, and honor one another. If you stumble into sin, there is always abundant grace and forgiveness. God is the God of second chances!

Homework - Part 2

PARENTS: An invaluable part of the purity study is to choose a book on sexual purity (age appropriate for your specific child) and have this book be part of the homework for this character trait. This will coincide with the mentor who is chosen. The recommendation is for the mentor to go through the book with your child. Since the process of completing a study guide would take several months (if your child meets weekly with a mentor) this would be done simultaneously alongside the study of other character traits.

Due to the length of time, if you chose a book study with a mentor, it is recommended that Sexual Purity be studied toward the beginning of the curriculum to allow time to thoroughly complete it and allow for missed mentor weeks. If you prefer, the study guide can be the only homework assigned for the sexual purity trait without requiring other homework questions. Reference the resource guide in Part Four of this book for sexual purity study guide resources.

Historical Figure

Choose a person from history (past or present) whom you feel exhibits qualities of sexual purity. You may choose from the list provided in the resource guide in Party Four of this book or select one of your own. Do some research on this person (internet search, library books) and answer the following questions:

1. Why did you choose this individual?

2. What aspect of sexual purity do they exhibit?

3. Explain how they lived this out in their daily life.

4. What obstacles, if any, did they have to overcome to remain pure?

5. Did they ever give in to temptation and need to deal with repentance and forgiveness?

Biography/Autobiography

If you like to read, select a biography or autobiography on this individual to read throughout this month. Your parent may ask you to provide a book report or synopsis (personal choice for format) on what you read, paying special attention to their commitment to purity.

 **Media Option**

Is there a movie or documentary on the historical figure you chose? If so, take some time to watch it and write down several things you can identify about their life of purity (or their commitment to return to purity).

 **Mentoring**

Choose a mentor who you and your parent(s) are comfortable sharing about sexual purity. For boys, a male youth pastor or godly college age friend is a great idea. For girls, a trusted college age or older babysitter, family friend, or female youth leader is recommended. Select a book you feel most closely represents your family values. Ask the mentor to decide, along with your child, how often they will meet to discuss the chapter and questions. If the mentor is not local, videoconferencing works well for mentor meetings. If your mentor provides charts, lists, or diagrams as visuals, insert them into your binder for this chapter, along with any notes you may take.

If your mentor is willing, encourage them to share their own victories or pitfalls with sexual purity/immorality.

If you need suggestions for purity study guides, reference the resource pages in Part Four of this book.

Journal Page

1. What, if anything, did the Lord imprint on your heart during your study of purity?

2. What are your thoughts and questions about this topic?

3. Do you struggle with any kind of sexual immorality (watching pornography, physical boundaries with a boyfriend or girlfriend…)? There is freedom in being honest with yourself and with a parent. Maybe a pastor or youth leader is willing to talk with you and help you work towards forgiveness. (No written response is required).

4. Spend some time in prayer talking to God about what you have learned from this study and the lessons you learned from your mentor.

5. Review your memory verse.

Purity Ring Discussion Page

A special way to commemorate your child's commitment to sexual purity is with the presentation of a purity ring at the end of this chapter study. When a ring is presented to your son or daughter and placed on their left-hand ring finger, you are expressing your desire for them to remain sexually pure until their wedding night. Your child wears the ring to honor their commitment to you as their parent(s) but more importantly, it is a visible representation of their commitment to the Lord, much the same as the symbol of the wedding ring. The purity ring is replaced by the engagement ring (for the girl) or wedding ring (for the guy). A constant visual reminder helps our kids recall their commitment to purity.

As parents, discuss with each other what you want the presentation of the ring to your son or daughter to look like. For our family, my husband and I took our daughter to a remote location with walking paths through brush and beautiful trees. We found a large tree with low trunks and had our daughter sit on the trunk while her dad, mostly, read some scriptures about purity and talked about our desires for her. He placed the ring on her finger, and we prayed together, committing her to the Lord. For our son, we went to the park across the street and sat on a picnic table and shared much the same experience, scriptures, our desires, and prayer. Both were meaningful and personal to our unique children.

Choose a ring your son or daughter would like. Get their input to ensure it is a style they will enjoy wearing on their finger and make sure it is sized properly. You may want to have the inside of the ring engraved. That is optional.

Resources for where to find rings are listed in Part Four of the resource guide. The following questionnaire is provided for you to write down your ideas for rings and presentation.

QUESTIONNAIRE:

1. What type of ring does my son/daughter like?

2. Do we want to engrave it? If so, what is the message?

3. How and where do we want to present it?

4. Date of presentation?

5. Scriptures we want to read when we present the ring:

6. Prayer of blessing and commitment:

Alternative Learning Pages
Do all or some of the following 7 activities

Activity 1 – Read, or have someone read to you, the verses for sexual purity in the Scripture study at the beginning of this chapter. Make a list of all the things you hear that showed Joseph's commitment to honor God.

_____   _____

_____   _____

_____   _____

_____   _____

Activity 2 – Read, or have someone read to you, the verses for sexual purity in the Scripture study at the beginning of this chapter. Why does God speak so highly of marriage? What are some of the consequences of having sex outside of marriage?

_____

_____

_____

Activity 3 – Read, or have someone read to you, the story of David in 2 Samuel 11. Fill in the chart below listing the poor decisions David made with Bathsheba in the first column. In the second column, write what he should have done instead.

David's Poor Choices	The Better Choice

Activity 4

1. What were the consequences of David's sin? Reference 2 Samuel 12:13, 14.

2. What was David's response after hearing his child had died in 2 Samuel 12:20? Why did he respond this way?

3. After David's sin with Bathsheba, did God disqualify him from doing anything further for God? Explain your answer. Use 2 Samuel 21:15-22 and 1 Kings 2:4 to form your answer.

Activity 5 – Temptation will hit all of us on various levels and in different ways throughout our lifetime. Some temptations will be easier to resist than others. With the help of a parent or sibling if you need it, come up with a scenario in which a person is tempted to sin sexually. Generate two endings, one in which the person gives in to the temptation, showing the results of their choice, and one in which the person flees from the temptation, and the benefit of their choosing purity. Write, or have someone write for you, on a separate sheet of paper and insert it into your binder for this chapter.

Activity 6 – If you like to draw, illustrate the two different endings above, showing the difference between giving in to sexual sin and resisting sexual sin. Drawings could be of faces, or using color to represent different choices, or writing words in different fonts and sizes to represent the opposing results. When completed, insert your drawing into your binder for this chapter.

Activity 7 – As a young person, what decisions and/or boundaries about purity can you make now to help you when you are tempted later? Use the questions below to help guide your answers. Put one answer in each box.

1. What will I decide about being alone with the opposite sex late at night?
2. If I am in a tempting situation that feels uncomfortable, what will I do?
3. I would like to remain a virgin until I am married because…
4. My body is a temple of the Holy Spirit. I will honor it, and others by …
5. Who will help keep me accountable with these choices?

Chapter Three

Discipline vs. Laziness

MONTHLY PLANNING PAGE

MONTH _____   CHARACTER TRAIT _____   PITFALL _____

HOMEWORK SECTION   COMPLETED   MENTOR _____
(insert on each line below the homework sections you will complete for this trait)

WEEK 1
☐ ☐ ☐ ☐   DATES WE MEET _____
_____
_____   MEMORY VERSE _____
_____   HISTORICAL FIGURE _____

WEEK 2
☐ ☐ ☐ ☐   BIOGRAPHY/AUTOBIOGRAPGY TITLE (if applicable) _____
_____
_____   SEXUAL PURITY STUDY GUIDE TITLE (if applicable) _____
_____

WEEK 3
☐ ☐ ☐ ☐   SERVICE PROJECTS (if applicable) _____
_____
_____
_____   DATES PROJECTS COMPLETED _____

WEEK 4
☐ ☐ ☐ ☐
_____
_____   NOTES, PAPERS, RESEARCH INSERTED IN BINDER:
_____
_____   YES   NO

Godly Trait – Discipline

The dictionary gives this definition for discipline - activity, exercise, or a regimen that develops or improves a skill; training. (3) For the purposes of this character study, we will look at two forms of discipline: spiritual and physical. The Bible has plenty to say about both.

Spiritual Discipline

Spiritual discipline creates in us a desire to not only spend time in God's Word but also with God's people. We want to grow up knowing what the Bible says and how it can guide our decisions in life. Spiritual discipline can include:
- Bible reading habits
- Scripture memory habits
- Prayer life
- Attending church/youth group

Scripture Study

Psalm 119:105
Your word is a lamp to my feet and a light to my path.

Joshua 1:8
This Book of the Law shall not depart from your mouth, but you shall meditate on it day and night, so that you may be careful to do according to all that is written in it. For then you will make your way prosperous, and then you will have good success.

Hebrews 4:12
For the word of God is living and active, sharper than any two-edged sword, piercing to the division of soul and of spirit, of joints and of marrow, and discerning the thoughts and intentions of the heart.

Psalm 119:11
I have stored up your word in my heart, that I might not sin against you.

Psalm 54:2
Hear my prayer, O God; listen to the words of my mouth.

Hebrews 10:24-25
And let us consider how we may spur one another on toward love and good deeds, not giving up meeting together, as some are in the habit of doing, but encouraging one another...

Physical Discipline

We want to adopt a healthy lifestyle and to take care of our bodies because they belong to the Holy Spirit. We want to understand that an active lifestyle is not only good for our bodies, but also needed for emotional and mental health. Physical disciplines can include:
- Eating habits
- Exercise

Scripture Study

1 Corinthians 6:19-20
Do you not know that your bodies are temples of the Holy Spirit, who is in you, whom you have received from God? You are not your own; you were bought at a price. Therefore, honor God with your bodies.

Daniel 1:8
But Daniel resolved not to defile himself with the royal food and wine, and he asked the chief official for permission not to defile himself this way.

Biblical Figure Study

Daniel – Daniel 1:8-16
But Daniel resolved that he would not defile himself with the king's food, or with the wine that he drank. Therefore, he asked the chief of the eunuchs to allow him not to defile himself. And God gave Daniel favor and compassion in the sight of the chief of the eunuchs, and the chief of the eunuchs said to Daniel, "I fear my lord the king, who assigned your food and your drink; for why should he see that you were in worse condition than the youths who are of your own age? So you would endanger my head with the king." Then Daniel said to the steward whom the chief of the eunuchs had assigned over Daniel, Hananiah, Mishael, and Azariah, "Test your servants for ten days; let us be given vegetables to eat and water to drink. Then let our appearance and the appearance of the youths who eat the king's food be observed by you, and deal with your servants according to what you see." So he listened to them in this matter, and tested them for ten days. At the end of ten days it was seen that they were better in appearance and fatter in flesh than all the youths who ate the king's food. So the steward took away their food and the wine they were to drink and gave them vegetables.

When Daniel was taken captive by the Babylonians, he along with his three friends, were chosen to be set apart for the king's palace, trained in all matters of wisdom, knowledge, and literature of the culture. They would ultimately serve the king. They were given the king's food to enjoy. Daniel knew he was set apart before God and did not want to dishonor him by eating food that was unclean.

Pitfall – Laziness

A lazy child becomes an adult with no work ethic who is unable to handle responsibility. It is important to learn the value of hard work.

Benjamin Franklin put it simply, "Idol hands are the devil's playthings." [4] What that means is that if we allow a lifestyle of laziness (being idle), we open ourselves up for bad habits and negative behaviors.

Scripture Study

Proverbs 12:24
Diligent hands will rule, but laziness ends in forced labor.

Proverbs 19:15
Laziness brings on deep sleep, and the shiftless go hungry.

Proverbs 10:4
Lazy hands make for poverty, but diligent hands bring wealth.

Biblical Figure Study

There is not a particular lazy person the Bible calls out. However, plenty of characteristics are provided about the sluggard, lazy person. Study Proverbs 24:30-34 below.

"I went past the field of a sluggard, past the vineyard of someone who has no sense; thorns had come up everywhere, the ground was covered with weeds, and the stone wall was in ruins. I applied my heart to what I observed and learned a lesson from what I saw: A little sleep, a little slumber, a little folding of the hands to rest – and poverty will come on you like a thief and scarcity like an armed man."

Discipline vs. Laziness Homework

1. In the story of Daniel above, explain how he showed discipline in his attitude toward the king's food.

2. Do you think the choice not to defile himself was a split-second decision or was it a decision he made prior to captivity? Explain the basis for his choice.

3. Is discipline easy to attain? What does discipline require?

4. In what areas are you already showing qualities of discipline? Where do you need improvement?

5. Do any of the verses that speak to laziness resonate with you and your behavior or attitude? Explain.

6. Proverbs 24:30-34 talk about the lazy man. What characteristics do you see?

7. How do you see God being honored through your discipline? How do you see your laziness as a hindrance in your relationship with him?

8. Memorize one of the Scripture verses listed above on godly discipline (either spiritual or physical). Reference the verse you chose.

Becoming a Woman of Discipline

Hey gals, the following questions are just for you. Take some time to work through them, being as honest as you can.

All of us come in various shapes and sizes. We are made with different bone structure: some of us are tall or short, skinny, or more muscular. Some of us gain weight quickly, while others could eat ice cream and donuts all day and not gain a pound. There is no one-fits-all approach when it comes to being healthy, so there should not be a one-size fits-all approach to physical fitness. We read in the Scripture study that our bodies are a temple of the Holy Spirit. We are to take care of what God gave us, because we only get one body in our lifetime. Body image can be a tough thing at your age, as girls are always comparing how they look to either other girls or the images portrayed on social media.

1. What is your biggest struggle when it comes to body image and comparisons?

2. Are there ways you can take better care of your body with the focus being on health rather than on looking like someone else? Can you change your focus to be on developing disciplined habits, approaching it from a positive perspective rather than the negative? How will you do that?

3. Spiritual discipline will become an important need the older you get. Life will become complicated and sometimes painful. You will experience joys and sorrows on a regular basis. Knowing where your strength comes from will be crucial for you as a godly woman. What kind of example as an adult woman will you want to set for those coming after you when it comes to spiritual practices? What kind of spiritual habits do you want to have?

In adulthood you will be grateful you learned how to live a disciplined life as a young person. Creating strong spiritual and physical discipline habits will enable you to guide your future family. It can help you enable coworkers or employees to establish healthy work/life boundaries. It can help you establish an expected work ethic in ministry or volunteering. A disciplined woman honors the Lord as she commits her goals and efforts to him.

Becoming a Man of Discipline

Hey guys, the following questions are just for you. Take some time to work through them, being as honest as you can.

1. With the goal of reaching manhood in a godly and biblical way, we have chosen a strong male figure, Daniel, to study. Can you think of other men in the Bible who are good examples of discipline? Why is it important as a young man to learn discipline in both spiritual and physical habits?

2. You may need to fight the tendency to be lazy when you are an adult. You may have a difficult job that leaves you mentally or physically exhausted. Rest is critical to help you recover your energy so you can do the things that are important to you. But laziness can easily creep in and prevent you from fulfilling responsibilities, such as a family or ministry. What commitments will you make now, regarding spiritual and physical discipline, that you will want to maintain when you are a man? Write out how you will establish these habits. Sign it and date it.

In adulthood you will be grateful you learned how to live a disciplined life as a young person. Creating strong spiritual and physical discipline habits will enable you to guide your future family. It can help you enable coworkers or employees to establish healthy work/life boundaries. It can help you establish an expected work ethic in ministry or volunteering. A disciplined man honors the Lord as he commits his goals and efforts to him.

Historical Figure

Choose a person from history (past or present) whom you feel exhibits qualities of spiritual or physical discipline. You may choose from the list provided in the resource guide in Part Four of this book or select one of your own. Do some research on this person (internet search, library books) and answer the following questions:

1. Why did you choose this individual?

2. What aspect of discipline do they exhibit?

3. Explain how they lived this out in their daily life.

4. What obstacles did they have to overcome to maintain a disciplined life?

5. List any ways they were undisciplined prior to choosing a life of discipline, if applicable.

Biography/Autobiography

If you like to read, select a biography or autobiography on this individual to read throughout this month. Your parent may ask you to provide a book report or synopsis (personal choice for format) on what you read, paying special attention to your subject's life of discipline.

Media Option

Is there a movie or documentary on the historical figure you chose? If so, take some time to watch it and write down several things you can identify about their life of discipline.

Mentoring

Choose a mentor who exhibits qualities of discipline that you or your parent(s) admire. Get together (how often is up to you, but often one meeting is sufficient as there are many other mentors involved in this process) and listen as they share their life experiences with you. Your parents will help guide the content of your discussions along with your mentor's ideas. If your mentor provides charts, lists, or diagrams as visuals, insert them into your binder for this chapter, along with any notes you may take. Possible discussion questions may include:
- Things I did to become a disciplined person were…
- My quiet time with the Lord includes…
- How I practice this daily…
- Ways I stay physically fit are…

Journal Page

1. What, if anything, did the Lord imprint on your heart during your study of discipline?

2. From the homework page, did you identify any areas in your life of discipline that needed improvement? Or a need to change lazy habits? If so, what action steps might you take to make improvements?

3. What are you willing to give up to obtain discipline in these areas?

4. Spend some time in prayer talking to God about what you have learned, including the lessons you learned from your mentor.

5. Review your memory verse.

Alternative Learning Pages
Do all or some of the following 7 activities

Activity 1 - Make a list of good foods and healthy exercises/physical activity you can reasonably adopt for one month. Fill in the chart at the end of this chapter and check off the days you ate well and did some sort of physical activity. At the end of the month evaluate your appetite, energy, and sleep patterns. Write down anything you notice that is a positive change.

Activity 2 - Study the passages in the scripture study above that talk about Daniel showing discipline with the king's food.

1. Circle the correct words that describe his attitude.

Courageous	Determined
Fearful	Resolute
Steadfast	Lazy
Wavering	Compromising

2. Look up two of these words and write out their meanings in your own words.

_____

_____

Activity 3 - Read, or have someone read for you, the following scenario.

You have decided that you would like to run a marathon to raise money for schoolbooks for underprivileged kids in Bangladesh. You like to stay physically active, but you have never run a race this long before. The marathon is in six months. It is important to train your body to be able to run at this capacity. You will need to start out slow and pace yourself, so you do not get injured. Training at this level takes discipline.

1. Write out, or have someone write for you, how you would go about training. Think through things like food intake, type of food, running schedule, workout schedule, sleep schedule.

_____

_____

2. Would this type of training be easy or hard? Explain your answer.

3. What would make the process easier?

Activity 4 –

1. Have you ever been lazy? If so, describe what that is like for you.

2. Would you enjoy being lazy for a long period of time or would you prefer to have periodic responsibility or work to do? Why or why not?

3. Do you know someone who is disciplined in their work? Describe their attitude. Does their attitude resemble Daniel's?

Activity 5 – Complete the following crossword puzzle by answering the questions below:

DOWN
1. The result of being lazy (Proverbs 10:4)
2. 2 words that describe moments set aside for Bible reading and prayer, a spiritual discipline
5. Daniel's choice food
6. A spiritual discipline, talking to God
8. Another word for lazy
9. To hold firmly to what you believe

ACROSS
3. What Daniel received from God for his obedience
4. How God views our bodies, the house for the Holy Spirit
7. The kind of lifestyle we should adopt
8. God's word
10. Giving up pleasures or comforts for something you value
11. Committed to achieving a goal and pursuing it
12. To pollute, mar, or spoil
13. Unmotivated to work or achieve
14. He was obedient to God's command
15. Daniel was trained in this

Activity 6 – If you do not already have an established time set aside each day to read your Bible and talk to God, set up a schedule for one month and commit to doing that before you start your day or before you go to bed. Do it at a time that best suits your attention span and schedule. Use the chart below to create a check off list.

Day of the Week 1	Bible Reading	Prayer
Monday		
Tuesday		
Wednesday		
Thursday		
Friday		
Saturday		
Sunday		
Day of the Week 2	Bible Reading	Prayer
Monday		
Tuesday		
Wednesday		
Thursday		
Friday		
Saturday		
Sunday		
Day of the Week 3	Bible Reading	Prayer
Monday		
Tuesday		
Wednesday		
Thursday		
Friday		
Saturday		
Sunday		
Day of the Week 4	Bible Reading	Prayer
Monday		
Tuesday		
Wednesday		
Thursday		
Friday		
Saturday		
Sunday		

Activity 7 – Find a verse in the Scripture study section on discipline and write it out on a notecard. Put it somewhere you will see it and read it every day. Pray that the Lord gives you a disciplined heart.

Activity 1 Chart

Day of the Week 1	Healthy Food	Activity
Monday		
Tuesday		
Wednesday		
Thursday		
Friday		
Saturday		
Sunday		
Day of the Week 2	Healthy Food	Activity
Monday		
Tuesday		
Wednesday		
Thursday		
Friday		
Saturday		
Sunday		
Day of the Week 3	Healthy Food	Activity
Monday		
Tuesday		
Wednesday		
Thursday		
Friday		
Saturday		
Sunday		
Day of the Week 4	Healthy Food	Activity
Monday		
Tuesday		
Wednesday		
Thursday		
Friday		
Saturday		
Sunday		

Results:

Chapter Four

Compassion vs. Indifference

MONTHLY PLANNING PAGE

MONTH _____ CHARACTER TRAIT _____ PITFALL _____

HOMEWORK SECTION   COMPLETED
(insert on each line below the homework sections you will complete for this trait)

WEEK 1
_____   ☐ ☐ ☐ ☐
_____

WEEK 2
_____   ☐ ☐ ☐ ☐
_____

WEEK 3
_____   ☐ ☐ ☐ ☐
_____

WEEK 4
_____   ☐ ☐ ☐ ☐
_____

MENTOR _____

DATES WE MEET _____
_____

MEMORY VERSE _____

HISTORICAL FIGURE _____

BIOGRAPHY/AUTOBIOGRAPGY TITLE (if applicable) _____

SEXUAL PURIITY STUDY GUIDE TITLE (if applicable) _____

SERVICE PROJECTS (if applicable) _____
_____

DATES PROJECTS COMPLETED _____
_____

NOTES, PAPERS, RESEARCH INSERTED IN BINDER:

YES   NO

Godly Trait – Compassion

A compassionate person is aware of the needs of those around them and does what they can to meet them. Often compassion involves sacrifice, giving to help those who do not have the resources we have. We want to have soft hearts that break for what breaks God's heart. Areas of focus for this study will be:
- Compassion toward those who are in need (physical needs, financial needs)
- Compassion toward those who are hurting (disease/physical pain, mental illness, grief/loss)

Scripture Study

Ephesians 4:32
Be kind and compassionate to one another, forgiving each other, just as in Christ God forgave you.

Colossians 3:12
Therefore, as God's chosen people, holy and dearly loved, clothe yourselves with compassion, kindness, humility, gentleness, and patience.

1 Peter 3:8
Finally, all of you, be like-minded, be sympathetic, love one another, be compassionate and humble.

Biblical Figure Study

The Good Samaritan - Luke 10:29-37
*But he wanted to justify himself, so he asked Jesus, "And who is my neighbor?" In reply Jesus said: "A man was going down from Jerusalem to Jericho, when he was attacked by robbers. They stripped him of his clothes, beat him and went away, leaving him half dead. A priest happened to be going down the same road, and when he saw the man, he passed by on the other side. So too, a Levite, when he came to the place and saw him, passed by on the other side. But a Samaritan, as he traveled, came where the man was; and when he saw him, he took pity on him. He went to him and bandaged his wounds, pouring on oil and wine. Then he put the man on his own donkey, brought him to an inn and took care of him. The next day he took out two denarii and gave them to the innkeeper. 'Look after him,' he said, 'and when I return, I will reimburse you for any extra expense you may have.'
"Which of these three do you think was a neighbor to the man who fell into the hands of robbers?" The expert in the law replied, "The one who had mercy on him." Jesus told him, "Go and do likewise."*

This character did something counter-cultural. Samaritans were considered by Jews to be outcasts. They were looked down upon and shunned. This Samaritan man showed compassion to a stranger who might have even been a Jew (Scripture does not tell us).

Jesus – Mark 3:1-6
Another time Jesus went into the synagogue, and a man with a shriveled hand was there. Some of them were looking for a reason to accuse Jesus, so they watched him closely to see if he would heal him on the Sabbath. Jesus said to the man with the shriveled hand, "Stand up in front of everyone." Then Jesus asked them, "Which is lawful on the Sabbath: to do good or to do evil, to save life or to kill?" But they remained silent. He looked around at them in anger and, deeply distressed at their stubborn hearts, said to the man, "Stretch out your hand." He stretched it out, and his hand was completely restored. Then the Pharisees went out and began to plot with the Herodians how they might kill Jesus.

The best example of all is Christ himself. His whole life was lived showing compassion to others, such as widows, prostitutes, the sick, and children. His compassion was often met with resistance, mainly by the Pharisees who always found fault with what he did.

Pitfall – Indifference

"If it doesn't affect me, I don't care." This is an indifferent way of viewing the world around us. God wants us to engage the world, think deeply, and stand for something. Indifference and selfishness can go hand in hand in this example.

 ## Scripture Study

Revelation 3:16
So, because you are lukewarm – neither hot nor cold – I am about to spit you out of my mouth.

Isaiah 29:13
The Lord says: "These people come near to me with their mouth and honor me with their lips, but their hearts are far from me. Their worship of me is based on merely human rules they have been taught."

 # Biblical Figure Study

<u>The Good Samaritan</u> - Read Luke 10:29-37 on the previous page.

The two people who did not show compassion, or were indifferent to the man's suffering were the priest and the Levite. The man's suffering and his wounds were obvious, yet they walked by on the other side, choosing not to help.

Compassion vs. Indifference Homework

1. What lesson from the Good Samaritan is applicable to you today?

2. What did this act of compassion cost the Samaritan?

3. When Jesus showed compassion, the Pharisees had a hard time accepting it. Why do you think that is?

4. When have you shown compassion? When have you not, but should have? Why is it sometimes hard to be compassionate?

5. Reread Revelation 3:16 and study why being lukewarm is displeasing to God. Jot down some ideas. You can do an internet study from a reliable Christian website or simply study the meaning from a study Bible or concordance in the back of your Bible.

6. What might our indifference as Christians communicate to a world that needs our engagement and care?

7. Choose one of the verses on compassion and commit it to memory. Reference the verse you chose here and record it on your monthly planning page.

Becoming a Woman of Compassion:

Hey gals, the following questions are just for you. Work through them, being as honest as you can.

1. At the beginning of this chapter there were two kinds of compassion listed as part of this discussion. There is compassion for those who are in some sort of physical or financial need (someone might not have a car and cannot get to work, or they have more expenses this month than they do paycheck). There is compassion for those who are hurting or in pain (physical pain or emotional pain due to a heartache or loss). If we want to grow up to be godly women who are compassionate to those around us, we need to grow our "awareness muscles" and be alert to see where the needs are. Take some time this week and observe. While you are traveling to school or church, running errands, walking in your neighborhood, listening to conversations with your friends, look and listen to see if you become more aware of needs in the lives of people around you. After observing for a week, pray about what you have seen and heard and ask the Lord to nudge you in a few ways you can help. Write down one or two ways you can show compassion to those people.

2. When you are an adult, you want to have developed a soft heart toward others, to see needs and be drawn to help, rather than turning a blind eye to the helpless. Scripture has some excellent examples of compassionate women who helped others. Ruth had compassion on her mother-in-law, Naomi, and offered to stay with her after the death of both of their husbands. She could have returned to her family but chose to be a companion to Naomi who had lost both her sons and her husband. The woman at Zarephath showed compassion on Elijah who came to her needing a place to stay. She was poor and did not have enough to even feed herself yet she trusted the Lord to

provide for her so she could provide for Elijah. As a result of her compassion and trust, God multiplied her food supply. What kind of compassionate woman would you like to be? Give some examples or scenarios.

_____

_____

_____

Often compassion requires that we put our desires behind the needs of others. It can be inconvenient to love others as they need. It requires sacrifice and time that we may not have. Always seek the Lord for where he wants you to get involved. He will always equip you and provide the means to do what is required.

Becoming a Man of Compassion:

Hey guys, the following questions are just for you. Take the time to work through them, and be as honest as you can.

1. Have you heard it said that real men do not cry? That is the furthest thing from the truth. Jesus cried! It is important as young men that you develop a soft heart when it comes to recognizing the hurting people around you. Understanding that there are people who live differently, who have less, who have significant hurts and needs, creates compassion that Jesus desires. His heart broke. Are there things you are passionate about when it comes to needs in the world? Give a few examples.

   _____

   _____

   _____

2. As a guy, have you ever been mocked for showing compassion to someone, whether at school or on a sports team? Sometimes being compassionate can be met with ridicule. Boys who want to make themselves look popular or cool like to make fun of other boys who show compassion or are kind to the "unpopular." If this has ever happened to you, how did it feel and did it deter you from reaching out to the unpopular or hurting friend?

   _____

   _____

   _____

If you have not experienced ridicule for being tender-hearted and compassionate, keep an eye out for others who are and be an advocate. Stand up for injustice and be a voice for the voiceless! Start being more aware of the needs around you and pray that the Lord nudges you toward those needs that he would like you to meet. You cannot help everyone so do not try. But you can do something. Start building your "awareness muscles" and strive to be a godly man of compassion.

Historical Figure

Choose a person from history (past or present) whom you feel exhibits qualities of compassion. You may choose from the list provided in the resource guide in Part Four of this book or select one of your own. Do some research on this person (internet search, library books) and answer the following questions:

1. Why did you choose this individual?

2. What aspect of compassion do they exhibit?

3. Explain how they lived this out in their daily life.

4, Did their acts of compassion require sacrifice?

Biography/Autobiography

If you like to read, select a biography or autobiography on this individual to read throughout this month. Your parent may ask you to provide a book report or synopsis (personal choice on format) on what you read, paying special attention to your subject's commitment to compassion.

Media Option

Is there a movie or documentary on the historical figure you chose? If so, take some time to watch it and write down several things you can identify about their life of compassion.

Mentoring

Choose a mentor who exhibits qualities of compassion that you or your parent(s) admire. Do you know someone who likes to make meals for the sick or does hospital visits? Get together (how often is up to you, but often one meeting is sufficient as there are many other mentors involved in this process) and listen as they share their life experiences with you. Your parents will help guide the content of your discussions along with your mentor's ideas. If your mentor provides charts, lists, or diagrams as visuals, insert them into your binder for this chapter, along with any notes you may take. Possible discussion questions may include:
- How I developed a compassionate heart …
- Times I had to sacrifice to choose compassion were…
- Times I was ridiculed for being compassionate were…
- How I have been blessed through showing compassion…

Journal Page

1. What, if anything, did the Lord imprint on your heart during your study of compassion?

2. Do you consider yourself to be a compassionate person? What can you do to develop a softer heart toward the hurt and needy around you?

3. In what ways have you shown compassion? What was the result for you and for the other person?

4. Spend some time in prayer talking to God about what you have learned, including the lessons you learned from your mentor.

5. Review your memory verse.

Alternative Learning Pages
Do all or some of the following 7 activities

Activity 1 – Read, or have someone read to you, the godly trait, pitfall, and corresponding Scripture verses for this chapter. Do you understand the difference between compassion and indifference? Explain it in your own words.

_____

_____

Activity 2 - Read, or have someone read to you, Luke 10:29-38. Fill in the first row of the chart below (or have someone fill it in for you).

	How did they show compassion	Who did they show it to	Why did they have compassion
Good Samaritan			
Jesus			

Read or have someone read to you Mark 3:1-6. Fill in the second row of the chart above (or have someone fill it in for you).

Activity 3 – Read, or have someone read to you, the following scenario. Create two different endings (tell it to someone and have them be your scribe). One that shows indifference to the situation and one that shows compassion. Choose the ending that would most honor God. Would this be easy or hard to do? Why?

Danny and the Bully

Danny is a sweet kid. He is kind, funny and dependable. He likes to play with his blocks and build all sorts of amazing creations. He is very smart and can usually make something out of nothing. Danny has a disability that causes him to shuffle when he walks and not have good balance. He will often fall as his legs give out on him and many times, he has gotten hurt and broken an arm or wrist. To help prevent these falls he walks with a walker to give him stability. He can manage quite well on his own, though he is a bit slower getting to class than his friends as it takes him longer due to the shuffling. But his friends are patient with him, waiting for him down the hall so he does not go into class by himself. Danny likes to play sports after school with his buddies and they always allow modifications to the game so he can catch or shoot in his own time. Danny is generally a happy kid but there are some bullies at school that make life hard sometimes.

Joseph, the school bully, likes to trip Danny when he is walking because Danny will fall and make a scene. Kids will laugh. Joseph mocks Danny. Danny lays on the ground trying to get up. If his friends are around to help, they will scoop him up and get him balanced, but they are not always around, and that is when he is most vulnerable to Joseph's attacks.

One day, Danny must make the long trek from his locker to the field where he is meeting his buddies for a game of soccer. As he approaches the back door, he sees Joseph waiting for him behind a garbage can. Danny turns to walk the other way but Joseph, being faster and able-bodied, comes up behind him. Danny prays someone will show up to help him as he knows this will not end well.

Finish the story with two endings. One showing compassion and one showing indifference. Which one honors God? Is it easy or hard?

_____   _____

_____   _____

_____   _____

_____   _____

Activity 4 - If you like to draw, illustrate a scene from the above scenario on a separate piece of blank paper. Color it and then insert it into your binder for this chapter.

Activity 5 – Draw lines to match the phrase to either compassion or indifference

Ignoring needs around you

Honoring God

Compassion

It does not affect me why should I get involved

Walking on by

Sacrificing your time for others

Indifference

Your heart breaks for the hurting and needy

You do not have time to help

Helping when it is inconvenient

Activity 6 – Think of someone you know or see regularly with a physical or mental need who could use your compassion. Make a list of 3 ways you can be compassionate and do those things this month.

Name: _____

1. How I will show compassion:

_____

_____

_____

2. What were the results of my compassionate acts or words?

_____

_____

_____

Activity 7 – Can you recall a time when someone showed you compassion?

_____

1. What did they do?

_____

2. How did it make you feel? Explain.

_____

3. Has someone shown indifference toward you when you had a need?

_____

4. How did it make you feel? Explain.

_____

Pray and ask the Lord to give you a compassionate heart, to see what he needs you to see and view the world through his eyes.

Chapter Five

Integrity vs. Dishonor

MONTHLY PLANNING PAGE

MONTH _____   CHARACTER TRAIT _____   PITFALL _____

HOMEWORK SECTION   COMPLETED   MENTOR _____
(insert on each line below the homework sections you will complete for this trait)
                                                            DATES WE MEET _____
WEEK 1
_____ ☐ ☐ ☐ ☐   _____
_____   MEMORY VERSE _____
_____   HISTORICAL FIGURE _____

WEEK 2
_____ ☐ ☐ ☐ ☐   BIOGRAPHY/AUTOBIOGRAPGY TITLE (if applicable) _____
_____
_____   SEXUAL PURITY STUDY GUIDE TITLE (if applicable) _____

WEEK 3
_____ ☐ ☐ ☐ ☐   SERVICE PROJECTS (if applicable) _____
_____   _____
_____   _____

WEEK 4
_____ ☐ ☐ ☐ ☐   DATES PROJECTS COMPLETED _____
_____   _____
_____   NOTES, PAPERS, RESEARCH INSERTED IN BINDER:
                                                      YES   NO

Godly Trait – Integrity

The dictionary defines integrity as being honest and having strong moral principles, moral uprightness. It goes further to describe a state of being whole and undivided. [5] We want to be people with strong moral principles that do not waiver based on the situation. To be whole and undivided means that the whole of you, your public life and your private life, remains consistent and the same. It is a high calling to be known as a person of integrity.

Scripture Study

1 Kings 9:4
As for you, if you walk before me faithfully with integrity of heart and uprightness, as David your father did, and do all I command and observe my decrees and laws, I will establish your royal throne over Israel forever, as I promised David your father when I said, 'You shall never fail to have a successor on the throne of Israel.'

Psalm 25:21
May integrity and uprightness protect me, because my hope, LORD, is in you.

Proverbs 10:9
Whoever walks in integrity walks securely, but whoever takes crooked paths will be found out.

Provers 13:6
Righteousness guards the person of integrity, but wickedness overthrows the sinner.

Titus 2:7
In everything set them an example by doing what is good. In your integrity, seriousness and soundness of speech that cannot be condemned, so that those who oppose you may be ashamed because they have nothing bad to say about us.

Biblical Figure Study

Hannah – Read 1 Samuel 1

In this chapter we learn many things about Hannah. She is devoted to her husband, though he has a second wife. She does not retaliate in anger when Peninnah (wife #2) mocks her for not having children of her own. Hannah takes her sadness and grief to God in prayer. When God grants her desire for a baby, Hannah follows through on her promise to give her child back to God for his service in the temple. Hannah worships the Lord through it all.

Pitfall – Dishonor

Dishonor is the opposite of integrity or honor. If you dishonor someone you bring shame to them. If you are not an honorable person you are viewed as dishonest, untrustworthy, and shameful. Let us look at what the Bible says about dishonorable people.

 **Scripture Study**

Psalm 89:34
I will not violate (dishonor) my covenant or alter what my lips have uttered.

Proverbs 11:2
When pride comes, the comes disgrace (dishonor), but with humility comes wisdom.

Proverbs 18:3
When wickedness comes, so does contempt, and with shame (dishonor) comes reproach.

Romans 2:23
You who boast in the law, do you dishonor God by breaking the law?

 **Biblical Figure Study**

Achan – Read Joshua 6:17-19 below and Joshua 7 from your Bible or online Bible. Chapter 6 gives the background of the command that was to be followed and the disobedience of Achan in chapter 7.

The city and all that is in it are to be devoted to the LORD. Only Rahab the prostitute and all who are with her in her house shall be spared, because she hid the spies we sent. But keep away from the devoted things, so that you will not bring about your own destruction by taking any of them. Otherwise, you will make the camp of Israel liable to destruction and bring trouble on it. All the silver and gold and the articles of bronze and iron are sacred to the LORD and must go into his treasury.

Integrity vs. Dishonor Homework

1. Reread the story of Hannah in 1 Samuel 1. List all the things you can find that were reasons for her to be angry at God.

2. Instead of anger what was Hannah's response to God in her grief? Why was that possible?

3. How did Hannah show integrity when it came to Samuel and her vow to the Lord? Would this have been an easy decision?

4. What was it about Achan, in Joshua 6 and 7, that made it possible for him to dishonor the Lord and bring dishonor to the Israelites? What were the choices he made?

5. What are some ways you can build strong integrity? List 5 things (ex: being honest when you make a mistake and choosing not to cover it up or blame someone else).

6. What might be some consequences for having a lack of integrity or not being an honorable person? Think in terms of a job, in school, or with friends. Why does it matter?

7. Choose one of the verses from the integrity Scripture study and commit it to memory. Reference the verse you chose here and record it on your monthly planning page.

Integrity, though a stand-alone character trait in this curriculum, is the umbrella trait by which all the others exist. If you do not have integrity, it will be hard to show humility, honesty, discipline, sexual purity, etc. Becoming a man or woman of integrity takes practice. Have you heard the question, "Who are you when no one is looking?" When you are alone, or are somewhere where there are no adults to monitor your behavior and choices, what are the things you choose to do? How do you choose to entertain yourself? Do you follow the rules and boundaries set up by those in authority over you, even if they are not around to see? Or do you take advantage of being alone and try to get away with breaking the rules, watching that movie that is not appropriate, having the party, etc.? God is always watching—not to pounce on you when you do something wrong, but because he sees everything in his creation, all the time. He loves us too much to not be one hundred percent present for us.

Becoming a Woman of Integrity:

Hey gals, these questions are just for you. Take the time to work through them, being as honest as you can.

1. When you are alone, are you ever tempted to break the rules or stretch the boundary because no one will see or know? Share a time this happened and how did you feel afterward?

2. As you grow into womanhood, integrity will be of utmost importance. For women, we need integrity in how we dress: what kind of message are we sending by our appearance? In how we conduct ourselves in public: will people feel threatened by our behavior or feel safe? In how we speak about others: will people consider us gossips or trustworthy? Are any of these areas you can be working on now as a young lady so that when you are an adult you have built a solid foundation for integrity?

3. A good way to practice integrity is to ask a friend to keep you accountable. Confide in each other your areas of struggle and check in with one another periodically to see how you are doing. Help each other maintain boundaries and come alongside when you see signs of lack of integrity. Accountability is essential as you grow to adulthood. Having someone you can share everything with who will pray with you and keep you on track helps so much. Identify someone in your life right now who could be this person for you. Chat about how you can keep each other accountable and agree to the "rules" of this relationship. Some potential accountability questions for each other would be:
   - Did you abide by your parent's rules even when you were home alone?
     (If the answer is no, confess, pray together, and make things right with your parents.)
   - Is there anything you are keeping from me that you need to bring to light?

Accountability Partner

Accountability Rules

When my husband and I dated in college, we each had one friend who agreed to be our accountability partner. We were committed to sexual purity before marriage, so we wanted to make sure we set healthy boundaries in our physical relationship. To help us stick to those boundaries we decided that after every date we would check in with our accountability partners and share everything we did physically. To avoid embarrassing conversations, it kept us from going too far. This type of accountability is not for everyone, but it helped us maintain our integrity with each other.

Keep short accounts with the Lord. Every day, maybe at night before you got to sleep, ask the Lord to help you recall those things that need to be made right. Maybe you said something hurtful. Or you disobeyed your parents, and they did not know it. Did you break a trust that you need to make right? Keeping your heart soft to recognize your failings will help you establish a firm foundation of integrity that you will carry into adulthood.

Becoming a Man of Integrity:

Hey guys, these questions are just for you. Take the time to work through them, being as honest as you can.

1. When you are alone, are you ever tempted to break the rules or stretch the boundary because no one will see or know? Share a time this happened. How did you feel afterward?

2. As you grow into manhood, integrity will be of utmost importance. Your thought life, as we discussed in the sexual purity chapter guys' question number 4, plays a key role. It is hard to have integrity as a man if your thought life is contrary to what the Lord requires of us. Think through some potential work and home life situations you may find yourself

in as a man. How would integrity in your thoughts shape your choices and behaviors? Feel free to ask your dad or another adult male what they think.

3. A good way to practice integrity is to ask a friend to keep you accountable. Confide in each other your areas of struggle and check in with one another periodically to see how you are doing. Help each other maintain boundaries and come alongside when you see signs of lack of integrity. Accountability is essential as you grow to adulthood. Having someone you can share everything with who will pray with you and keep you on track helps so much. Identify someone in your life right now who could be this person for you. Chat about how you can keep each other accountable and agree to the "rules" of this relationship. Some potential accountability questions for each other would be:
   - Did you abide by your parent's rules even when you were home alone?
     (If the answer is no, confess, pray together, and make things right with your parents.)
   - Is there anything you are keeping from me that you need to bring to light?

Accountability Partner

Accountability Rules

When my husband and I dated in college, we each had one friend who agreed to be our accountability partner. We were committed to sexual purity before marriage, so we wanted to make sure we set healthy boundaries in our physical relationship. To help us stick to those boundaries we decided that after every date we would check in with our accountability partners and share everything we did physically. To avoid embarrassing conversations, it kept us from going too far. This type of accountability is not for everyone, but it helped us maintain our integrity with each other.

Keep short accounts with the Lord. Every day, maybe at night before you got to sleep, ask the Lord to help you recall those things that need to be made right. Maybe you said something hurtful. Or you disobeyed your parents, and they did not know it. Did you break a trust that you need to make right? Keeping your heart soft to recognize your failings will help you establish a firm foundation of integrity that you will carry into adulthood.

Historical Figure

Choose a person from history (past or present) whom you feel exhibits qualities of integrity. You may choose from the list provided in the resource guide in Part Four of this book or select one of your own. Do some research on this person (internet search, library books) and answer the following questions:

1. Why did you choose this individual?

2. What aspect of integrity do they exhibit?

3. Explain how they lived this out in their daily life.

4. What obstacles, if any, did they have to overcome to be a person of integrity?

5. Was there ever a time this person did not have integrity or showed qualities of dishonor? If yes, list some examples.

Biography/Autobiography

If you like to read, select a biography or autobiography on this individual to read throughout this month. Your parent may ask you to provide a book report or synopsis (personal choice for format) on what you read, paying special attention to your subject's life of integrity.

 # Media Option

Is there a movie or documentary on the historical figure you chose? If so, take some time to watch it and write down several things you can identify about their life of integrity.

 # Mentoring

Choose a mentor who exhibits qualities of integrity that you or your parent(s) admire. Get together (how often is up to you, but often one meeting is sufficient as there are many other mentors involved in this process) and listen as they share their life experiences with you. Your parents will help guide the content of your discussions along with your mentor's ideas. If your mentor provides charts, lists, or diagrams as visuals, insert them into your binder for this chapter, along with any notes you may take. Possible discussion questions may include:
- Ways I live out integrity at work are…
- Times I was not very honorable in my work, home, friendships were…
- Things I have had to sacrifice because I chose to be a person of honor are…

Journal Page

1. What, if anything, did the Lord imprint on your heart during your study of integrity?

2. Are you challenged in any way to work toward having more integrity in your life? If so, what areas?

3. What do you admire about your mentor's life of integrity?

4. Spend some time in prayer talking to God about what you have learned and ask him to help you build stronger integrity.

5. Review your memory verse.

Alternative Learning Pages
Do all or some of the following 8 activities

Activity 1 – Read, or have someone read to you, the godly trait, pitfall, and corresponding scriptures for each from the trait descriptions and Scripture study at the beginning of the chapter. Do you understand the difference between integrity and dishonor? Explain it in your own words.

_____

_____

Activity 2 – Make a list of all the qualities you can think of that a person of integrity might have. Write your answers in the blanks below or have someone write for you.

_____	_____
_____	_____
_____	_____
_____	_____

Activity 3 – In the story of Hannah in 1 Samuel 1, write, or have someone write for you, an alternative ending to what it says in Scripture. If she had been a dishonorable person, how would the story have turned out differently?

_____

_____

_____

Activity 4 – Draw lines from the word or phrase that goes with either Hannah or Achan

Bar of Gold		Silver
Devotion		Stoning
Devoted things	**Hannah**	Rival
Weeping	**Achan**	Offering
God's anger burned		Treasury
Temple		Given over to the Lord
Destruction		Priest

Activity 5 – In the story of Achan and the spoils, if it had been you, what would you have done? Is it an easy thing or a hard thing to leave those valuables behind?

Activity 6 – If you like to craft, create a piece of art that depicts the differences between Hannah and Achan. You can draw a picture, build something that symbolizes each character, paint using colors that represent integrity and dishonor as you imagine it. If using paper, insert your finished page into your binder for this chapter. If you build something, take a picture of it, print it, and insert it in your binder

Activity 7 – If you like digital media, create a stop motion video representing one of the above characters.

Activity 8 – Think of areas of integrity you need to work on. Reference your list in Activity 2. How can you build stronger integrity? Write your answer or tell a parent or sibling and have them record your ideas.

Chapter Six

Courage vs. Cowardice

MONTHLY PLANNING PAGE

MONTH _____ CHARACTER TRAIT _____ PITFALL _____

HOMEWORK SECTION COMPLETED MENTOR _____
(insert on each line below the homework sections you will complete for this trait)

WEEK 1
_____ ☐☐☐☐ DATES WE MEET _____
_____
_____ MEMORY VERSE _____
_____ HISTORICAL FIGURE _____

WEEK 2
_____ ☐☐☐☐ BIOGRAPHY/AUTOBIOGRAPGY TITLE (if applicable) _____
_____
_____ SEXUAL PURIITY STUDY GUIDE TITLE (if applicable) _____
_____

WEEK 3
_____ ☐☐☐☐ SERVICE PROJECTS (if applicable) _____
_____
_____
_____ DATES PROJECTS COMPLETED _____

WEEK 4
_____ ☐☐☐☐
_____
_____ NOTES, PAPERS, RESEARCH INSERTED IN BINDER:
_____
       YES _____ NO _____

Godly Trait – Courage

Being a person of courage is something we all should strive for. Throughout our lifetime we will need to be courageous in many different ways. We will need courage to stand up to evil and injustice. We will need to be courageous when we or a loved one is going through something hard or painful, or when we are tempted to do something we know is wrong. Talking about our faith to an unbeliever requires courage. Courage shows up when we are afraid, but still need to do the thing that is causing fear. Courage has many different faces, but they all show a godly character in us.

Author Mary Anne Radmacher wrote, "Courage doesn't always roar. Sometimes courage is the quiet voice at the end of the day saying, 'I will try again tomorrow.'" [6] Billy Graham was also known to say, "Courage is contagious. When a brave man takes a stand, the spines of others are often stiffened." [7]

Scripture Study

Joshua 1:9
Have I not commanded you? Be strong and courageous. Do not be afraid; do not be discouraged, for the LORD your God will be with you wherever you go.

1 Chronicles 19:13
Be strong, and let us fight bravely for our people and the cities of our God. The LORD will do what is good in his sight.

1 Corinthians 16:13
Be on your guard; stand firm in the faith; be courageous; be strong.

Philippians 1:20
I eagerly expect and hope that I will in no way be ashamed but will have sufficient courage so that now as always Christ will be exalted in my body, whether by life or by death.

# Biblical Figure Study

Esther – Read Esther 7

Leading up to chapter 7, we read in the previous chapters that Esther was chosen out of all the young women to be queen of Persia. Haman, the king's right-hand man, hated the Jews and devised a plan to have them exterminated. With the prayers of her people and the encouragement of her relative Mordecai, Esther, who was Jewish, mustered up the courage to approach the king and request that he save her people. She could have been killed for simply entering the king's throne room without being summoned. But she went further than that to present her request to him, revealing that she, too, was a Jew. Read chapter 7 to see what happened.

Pitfall – Cowardice

The opposite of being courageous is being a coward. Does that sound harsh? Because if I am afraid of something, I do not like to think I am being cowardly by not doing it. We usually reserve the word coward for individuals who do not stick up for the underdog, who run when things get hard, and choose not to do the right thing. It is true that those are appropriate illustrations of a coward. However, if we make the choice to live in fear rather than in faith, is it a fair description of our actions? Let's look at the Bible for help.

# Scripture Study

Genesis 26:7
When the men of that place asked him about his wife, he said, "She is my sister," because he was afraid to say, "She is my wife." He thought, "The men of this place might kill me on account of Rebekah, because she is beautiful."

Proverbs 28:1
The wicked flee though no one pursues but the righteous are as bold as a lion.

John 18:25
Meanwhile, Simon Peter was still standing there warming himself. So they asked him, "You aren't one of his disciples too, are you?" He denied it, saying, "I am not."

Revelation 21:8
But the cowardly, the unbelieving, the vile, the murderers, the sexually immoral, those who practice magic arts, the idolators and all liars — they will be consigned to the fiery lake of burning sulfur. This is the second death."

 **Biblical Figure Study**

Peter – Read John 18:15-27

Peter denies knowing Jesus because he is afraid of what they might do to him if he is associated with him. Rather than being truthful and risking his life for Christ he lies about his affiliation to save his own skin.

Courage vs. Cowardice Homework

1. In the story of Esther, what was the decision she had to make that required courage?

2. What was at risk for her? What were some possible outcomes?

3. Has there ever been a time in your life when a lot was riding on having courage to do something big? Describe it. What was the result?

4. Reread Joshua 1:9. Does it give you comfort knowing God is with you when you are afraid? It is okay to say no. Sometimes it is hard to feel God is with us since he is not a physical presence in our lives. In what ways does he show you he is near?

5. Can you relate to Peter's cowardice in John 18:15-27? Was there ever a time you chose the fearful path? Be honest. Describe the situation. All of us lose our courage from time to time.

6. Why does choosing courage over fear honor the Lord? Why is it important to him?

7. Choose a verse from the Scripture study above and commit it to memory. Reference the verse you chose below.

Becoming a Woman of Courage:

Hey gals, the following questions are just for you. Take some time to work through them, and be honest as you go.

1. As a young lady, in what areas do you find the most difficult to show courage? (Examples could be peer group pressures [girls can be mean], tempting situations with the opposite sex, admitting to wrongdoing such as cheating or lying, choosing modesty, sharing your faith, music choices).

2. Pick one area you just mentioned. Why is showing courage in this area so hard for you? Do you feel pressure from other girls to give in or keep this part of your life a secret?

3. What does it feel like for you to be pressured from your friends? Have you given in at times because it can be so hard to push against the pressure?

4. Can you think of a situation down the road, as you become a woman, where you will need to be courageous in the area that is currently a struggle for you? How will you want your older self to respond?

Peer pressure can make it difficult for young ladies who truly desire to make right choices and honor God. God has so much grace and forgiveness when we make choices that do not honor him. If you feel you have compromised where you should have been courageous, talk to God about that and let his forgiveness and grace wash over you. Ask him to give you the courage to make a different choice the next time that situation comes along. Believe me, there will always be a next time!

Becoming a Man of Courage:

Hey guys, the following questions are just for you. Take some time to work through them, and be honest as you go.

1. As a young man, in what areas do you find the most difficult to show courage? (Examples could be peer group pressures, crude joking—especially about girls, watching inappropriate content on TV or the internet, admitting to wrongdoing such as cheating or lying, tempting situation with the opposite sex, sharing your faith, music choices)

2. Pick one area you just mentioned. Why is showing courage in this area so hard for you? What outside influences make it easier to just give in than to stand up for what is right or what needs to be done? Do you find that guys your age tend to go with the crowd?

_____

_____

_____

3. If you are a guy who works hard to be a young man of courage, what can you do to encourage your peers who may struggle to stand up for purity, honesty, and truth? Who do you need to stand up and fight for? Build your leadership muscles and blaze a trail!

_____

_____

_____

Peer pressure can make it difficult for young men who truly desire to make right choices and honor Jesus. God has so much grace and forgiveness when we make choices that do not honor him. If you feel you have compromised where you should have been courageous, talk to God about that and let his forgiveness and grace wash over you. Ask him to give you the courage to make a different choice the next time that situation comes along. Believe me, there will always be a next time!

Historical Figure

Choose a person from history (past or present) whom you feel exhibits qualities of courage. You may choose from the list provided in Part Four of the resource section or select one of your own. Do some research on this person (internet search, library books) and answer the following questions:

1. Why did you choose this character?

2. What aspect of courage do they exhibit?

3. Explain how they lived this out in their daily life, or was it just specific moments?

4. What were the outcomes of their courageous choices? What, if anything, did they have to give up in order to be courageous?

5. Did they have moments of fear? Explain.

6. Could you do the acts of courage this person did? Why or why not?

Biography/Autobiography

If you like to read, select a biography or autobiography on this individual to read throughout this month. Your parent may ask you to provide a book report or synopsis (personal choice for format) on what you read, paying special attention to their courageous acts.

 # Media Option

Is there a movie or documentary on the historical person you chose? If so, take some time to watch it and write down several things you can identify about their life of courage?

 # Mentoring

Chose a mentor who exhibits qualities of courage that you or your parent(s) admire. Is there someone who has lived a difficult life with lots of loss, someone who has faced death, or had to stand up for righteousness and was persecuted for it? Get together (how often is up to you, but often one meeting is sufficient as there are many other mentors involved in this process) and listen as they share their life experiences with you. Your parents will help guide the content of your discussions along with your mentor's ideas. If your mentor provides charts, lists, or diagrams as visuals, insert them into your binder for this chapter, along with any notes you may take. Possible discussion questions may include:
- I had to be courageous when…
- Even though I showed courage I was still fearful. Things I did to help were…
- Results of my courage were…
- A time when I chose fear over courage was:..

Journal Page

1. What, if anything, did the Lord imprint on your heart during your study of courage?

2. What are your thoughts about the things your mentor shared regarding how they faced challenges that required courage?

3. Where do you need to show more courage in your life?

4. What part does fear play in courage?

5. Spend some time talking to Jesus. Tell him where you struggle, confess those times you allowed fear to replace courage, and renew your commitment to live courageously as a young man or woman of faith.

6. Review your memory verse.

Alternative Learning Pages
Do all or some of the following 8 activities

PLEASE NOTE ** It is important to recognize that some people have a diagnosed anxiety disorder which is an often constant and uncontrollable fear or worry. This makes it difficult to rationally think through a situation. For these people, and you may be one of them, they want to be courageous, but their mind is playing such tricks on them that they cannot choose anything different in the moment. In these situations, the person may require professional help to deal with severe anxiety. There are also tools and techniques a person can utilize to help overcome the fear in the moment. A counselor or trained professional can help them figure out ways to manage their anxiety and bring them to a place of better balance.

The activities and lessons on these pages are not intended to bring any kind of guilt to you if you are someone who struggles with an anxiety disorder. It is harder for you to overcome and may take more than simply praying for courage in the moment. As you work through the activities, take what you can from the lessons, see if there are things you can do to help you overcome your fear, and above all, Jesus is near. He sees you, is with you, and will always be your comfort no matter what you are anxious about.

Activity 1 – Read, or have someone read to you, the story of Esther starting in Esther 5. Summarize the story to a parent or sibling. Explain what led up to Esther starting her new position, what was the scary thing required of her, how did she respond to that situation, and what was the result.

Activity 2 – If you like to draw and color, draw a picture of Esther going before the king. Draw on a separate sheet of blank paper and insert it into your binder for this chapter.

Activity 3 – Think of a time when you were afraid. Write down, or have someone write for you, what the circumstance was. What did you do? Did you choose not to do something because you were too scared? Did you do the scary thing anyway? If you could go back and redo the "ending" to that situation, would you choose a different way to respond to your fear?

_____

_____

_____

_____

_____

Activity 4 – Read, or have someone read for you, the following scenario. Write, or tell someone, what some possible outcomes could be.

Jenny's Choice

Jenny was a sweet girl, age 13. She liked to hang out with her friends and listen to music. She was also an amazing artist. She always had an art project going. Jenny was a Christian and went to church with her family every Sunday. Often, she would bring friends with her to youth group. There were a few Christian kids at her school, but not many. Most of Jenny's friends did not believe as she did and sometimes things became tricky, but for the most part they got along well. There were times she did not attend some of their parties because her friends would watch things that were not acceptable or the behavior between the boys and the girls would get inappropriate. She often felt like she did not fit in and wished she could do the things her friends did even though she knew it was not right. Some days she was tired of always being the one who made the right choices.

    One weekend her parents allowed her to go to a mixed party. They knew the parents hosting the party and felt comfortable everything would stay appropriate. They had a conversation with Jenny before she left about their expectations for her. They trusted her to make the right choices if confronted with anything she knew went against their family values. They prayed with her before she left, then sent her on her way. While at the party, she met several new kids she had not seen before. Jenny enjoyed their company. They were funny and made her feel at ease. They talked about school and life and their parents. They all agreed their parents were too strict and had stupid rules. Though she did not feel the same way, Jenny chimed in so that she did not stand out or appear to be a "little goody two-shoes." She shared some stories of how her parents made her do things she thought were unreasonable and pretended to be angry with the rules that kept her from doing fun things. The kids listened and identified with her plight, and they began to bad-mouth their parents, suggesting ways they could rebel. Jenny started to feel uncomfortable after a while and felt a little stuck. She had been dishonest and disrespectful, two things she knew were wrong…

Think of a few ways this situation could end. Write out or have someone write for you your ideas, based on what you are learning about courage and cowardice.

Activity 5 – Read about Peter from John 18 and how he showed cowardly behavior. What might have happened to him if he had been honest about his association with Jesus? Do you think you would have had the same response? Has there been a time you pretended not to be a Christian because you were embarrassed to stand out? It is okay to be honest. We have all done it.

Activity 6 – If you like to design and build things with blocks, or any other type of craft, create something that shows an aspect of one of the Bible characters. It could be something that represents a choice they made, or a scene from the story. Explain it to a family member.

Activity 7 – Find all the words from the word bank in the word search below. Answers are in the answer key of Part Five of this book.

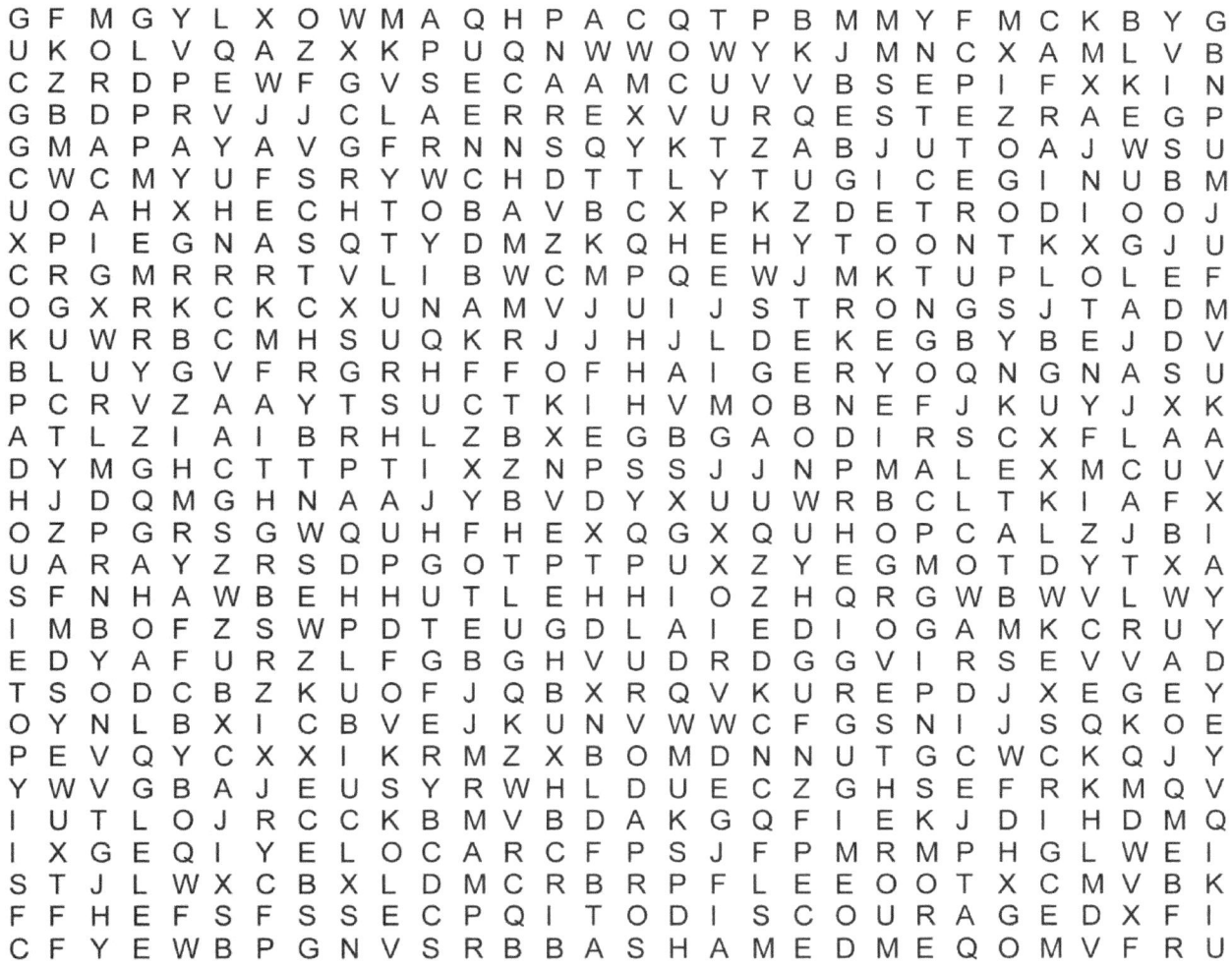

Esther	queen	Mordecai	Haman	Vashti
courageous	discouraged	Peter	cowardice	denial
fear	strong	faith	afraid	

Activity 8 – Select one of the Bible verses from either the godly trait of courage or the pitfall of cowardice and put it to memory using music, rap, a poem, or some other medium. Have a parent or sibling record it.

Chapter Seven

Self-Control vs. Self-Indulgence

MONTHLY PLANNING PAGE

MONTH _____ CHARACTER TRAIT _____ PITFALL _____

HOMEWORK SECTION   **COMPLETED**
(insert on each line below the homework sections you will complete for this trait)

WEEK 1
_____   ☐ ☐ ☐ ☐   MENTOR _____
_____   DATES WE MEET _____
_____   _____

WEEK 2
_____   ☐ ☐ ☐ ☐   MEMORY VERSE _____
_____   HISTORICAL FIGURE _____
_____   BIOGRAPHY/AUTOBIOGRAPGY TITLE (if applicable) _____

WEEK 3
_____   ☐ ☐ ☐ ☐   SEXUAL PURIITY STUDY GUIDE TITLE (if applicable) _____
_____   _____
_____   SERVICE PROJECTS (if applicable) _____
                                    _____

WEEK 4
_____   ☐ ☐ ☐ ☐   DATES PROJECTS COMPLETED _____
_____   _____
_____   NOTES, PAPERS, RESEARCH INSERTED IN BINDER:
                                              YES   NO

Godly Trait – Self Control

A self-controlled person is one who is aware of their own words and behavior and can keep themselves under control without the need of someone else doing it. A self-controlled person can control their appetites and keep a balanced way of life, choosing to wait rather than having something now. Self-control requires discipline. Ted Cunningham, author and pastor, says this, "Self-control is the discipline of delaying impulse or gratification for a greater purpose or cause. When we exercise self-control, we are saying 'no' for the sake of a bigger and better 'yes.' We are trading something in the here and now for something greater in the future." [8]

Scripture Study

Galatians 5:22-23
But the fruit of the Spirit is love, joy, peace, forbearance, kindness, goodness, faithfulness, gentleness, and self-control. Against such things there is no law.

1 Corinthians 6:12
"I have the right to do anything," you say – but not everything is beneficial. "I have the right to do anything" – but I will not be mastered by anything.

Romans 7:18
For I know that good itself does not dwell in me, that is, in my sinful nature. For I have the desire to do what is good, but I cannot carry it out.

Proverbs 25:27-28
It is not good to eat too much honey, nor is it honorable to search out matters that are too deep. Like a city whose walls are broken through is a person who lacks self-control.

Titus 2:11-12
For the grace of God has appeared that offers salvation to all people. It teaches us to say "No" to ungodliness and worldly passions, and to live self-controlled, upright, and godly lives in this present age.

2 Peter 1:5-8
For this very reason, make every effort to add to your faith goodness; and to goodness, knowledge; and to knowledge, self-control; and to self-control, perseverance; and to perseverance, godliness; and to godliness, mutual affection; and to mutual affection, love. For if you possess these qualities in increasing measure, they will keep you from being ineffective and unproductive in your knowledge of our Lord Jesus Christ.

 # Biblical Figure Study

Nehemiah – Read Nehemiah 4

Nehemiah oversaw the rebuilding of the walls around Jerusalem. Several enemies of the Jews made attempts to prevent their efforts, mocked them, and even plotted to kill them. Nehemiah was aware of their ridicule and attempts to impede their progress on the wall. Instead of shouting back at them or criticizing them, he stayed silent, prayed to God, and encouraged the Hebrews to continue to build. He told them to work with one hand and hold weapons in the other. The work would not be stalled. Nehemiah showed great restraint to stick to the job at hand and not get distracted by the threats around him.

David – Read 1 Samuel 24

When David was not yet king, he fled from King Saul who was trying to kill him. David's popularity as a military leader gained him more and more praise from the people, making Saul jealous. When David sought refuge deep inside a cave, Saul came into the entrance of the cave to rest. While Saul slept David could have killed him, but he respected Saul as the anointed king of Israel and showed restraint by only cutting off a piece of Saul's cloak. Vengeance or self-defense was at David's fingertips, but he chose self-control instead.

Daniel – Reread Daniel 1

You already studied the character of Daniel for the trait of discipline. There you learned how he refrained from eating the king's food in order not to defile himself. He was disciplined in what he put in his mouth and in taking care of his body. He was also being obedient to God. This same situation reveals the trait of self-control. The king's food was probably rich and delicious and looked very appetizing. He refrained from eating, instead choosing self-control to receive a future blessing from the Lord.

Pitfall – Self-Indulgence

The opposite of self-control is self-indulgence. This means you cannot control your own self and therefore need someone else to control you by correcting your behavior or speech. It also means you give in to your own appetites and desires and need immediate satisfaction and are unable to postpone your own wants.

Scripture Study

2 Timothy 3:1-5
But mark this: There will be terrible times in the last days. People will be lovers of themselves, lovers of money, boastful, proud, abusive, disobedient to their parents, ungrateful, unholy, without love, unforgiving, slanderous, without self-control, brutal, not lovers of the good, treacherous, rash, conceited, lovers of pleasure rather than lovers of God - having a form of godliness but denying its power. Have nothing to do with such people.

Proverbs 25:28
Like a city whose walls are broken through is a person who lacks self-control.

Provers 29:18
Where there is no revelation, people cast off restraint; but blessed is the one who heeds wisdom's instruction.

Biblical Figure Study

Samson – Judges 16:15-21
Then she said to him, "How can you say, 'I love you,' when you won't confide in me? This is the third time you have made a fool of me and haven't told me the secret of your great strength." With such nagging she prodded him day after day until he was sick to death of it. So he told her everything. "No razor has ever been used on my head," he said, "because I have been a Nazirite dedicated to God from my mother's womb. If my head were shaved, my strength would leave me, and I would become as weak as any other man." When Delilah saw that he had told her everything, she sent word to the rulers of the Philistines, "Come back once more; he has told me everything." So the rulers of the Philistines returned with the silver in their hands. After putting him to sleep on her lap, she called for someone to shave off the seven braids of his hair, and so began to subdue him. And his strength left him. Then she called, "Samson, the Philistines are upon you!" He awoke from his sleep and thought, "I'll go out as before and shake myself free." But he did not know that the LORD had left him. Then the Philistines seized him, gouged out his eyes and took him down to Gaza. Binding him with bronze shackles, they set him to grinding grain in the prison.

Samson, who was set apart by God, gave up the secret of his strength for the love of a woman. The result was eventually fatal. His lack of self-control cost him favor with God and then eventually his life.

<u>Adam and Eve</u> – Read Genesis 2

Adam and Eve walked and talked with God in the garden of Eden. When they were deceived by Satan, their desire for self-indulgence took over the command God gave them to have self-control: to not eat from the Tree of Knowledge of Good and Evil. That was the only thing they could not have, yet they wanted it. It looked satisfying and they wanted immediate gratification. Their sin of self-indulgence was also a sin of disobedience which then led to the sin of lying to cover up their original choice. The result was their banishment from the garden. Self-indulgence should not be viewed lightly.

<u>David</u> – Read 2 Samuel 11

David gave into the temptation with Bathsheba and as a result suffered deep consequence. The same situation shows a lack of self-control on his part. Rather than fleeing the temptation and the immediate gratification of sexual pleasure, he gave in to those desires. Not only did his lack of self-control effect his relationship with God, but it caused the death of his friend, the sorrow of Bathsheba, the death of their child, and disgrace to the Israelites. The lack of self-control can have severe consequences.

Self-Control vs. Self-Indulgence Homework

1. Review the biblical character stories above for both the godly trait and pitfall. Make a list comparing the self-controlled actions of David, Nehemiah, and Daniel, versus the self-indulgent actions of Samson, Adam/Eve and David. Is there a theme you can see for each? Write a sentence summarizing what you observe.

   Self-Controlled actions   Self-Indulgent actions

   _____   _____
   _____   _____
   _____   _____
   _____   _____
   _____   _____

   Summary   Summary

   _____   _____
   _____   _____

2. Read these specific passages from the Scripture study above: Daniel 2:14-18, Daniel 6:6-11, Nehemiah 4:4.

   A. What do you notice in these verses?

   B. What can we infer Daniel likely did, based on your answer above, before he asked if he and his friends could just eat vegetables instead of the king's food?

3. How important is prayer when it comes to self-control and why do we need to pray?

4. In what areas of your life do you exhibit self-control? Make a list on the lines in the first column below. In what areas are you self-indulgent or lacking self-control? Use the second column to record your answers. Think of one way you can work on having more self-control for each of the areas you list. For this whole month, work on these areas then record the results at the end of the month. Pray and ask God to help you in that effort.

Self-Control   **Self-Indulgent**

_____   _____

_____   _____

_____   _____

_____   _____

Ways I can work on self-control:

_____

_____

_____

Result:

_____

5. Why is it easier to self-indulge then to choose self-control? For Nehemiah, what might have been the outcome if he had chosen to chase after his tormentors and give them what they clearly deserved? How would that choice have possibly affected the rebuilding of the wall?

_____

_____

_____

6. Name some of the blessings that may come from living a self-controlled life. Is it worth it? Use Proverbs 25:28 from the Scripture study above to help you form your answer. What is the benefit of the "walls" in this passage?

_____

_____

7. Have you experienced any of the blessings you listed above because you chose self-control over self-indulgence? Explain.

8. Choose one of the verses on self-control and commit it to memory. Reference the verse you chose here and record it on your monthly planning page.

Becoming a Woman of Self-Control

Hey gals, the following questions are just for you. Take the time to work through them being as honest as you can.

1. Self-control could possibly be the most difficult of the traits. I find that often my physical desires overtake my ability to make right choices, or at least healthy choices. If I am hungry, I am more likely to grab a quick unhealthy snack rather than choose a healthier option. If I am upset, it is easier for me to spout off and react rather than taking the time to think through a more measured response. If I am tired, I am more likely to choose to stay on the couch than get up and exercise. Having the self-control to make better choices in whatever moment I find myself takes practice and we need it in every area of our lives. Can you think of ways self-control uniquely affects young women?

2. One way it might be hard for a girl to choose self-control is the area of the tongue. Holding your tongue when something hurtful has been done to you is not easy. Choosing not to say the hurtful thing back, choosing not to speak words of gossip, or putting someone down to make yourself look good, may take intentional action. Have you been in a situation where you wanted to use your tongue for harm but controlled it? Maybe you felt the need to defend yourself, but you should have let the moment pass? Share what happened.

3. A woman who lacks self-control is not someone the Lord wants you to be. Think about the consequences for a woman who walks down the path of self-indulgence. What do you think that might look like? Pray right now and commit to the Lord to surrender your desires to him and pursue self-control.

Becoming a Man of Self-Control

Hey guys, the following questions are just for you. Take the time to work through them, being as honest as you can.

1. What kind of negative thoughts come to mind when you think of the need to have self-control? "Uhh, I can't eat what I want," "I can't behave the way I want," "I can't watch certain movies," "I can't sit around the house all day." Seems very restrictive when you look at self-control through a negative lens. But what if you changed your perspective to think of the positive reasons to have limits on yourself? How would your outlook change if you saw your restrictions, your need for self-control, as a blessing? Think through the areas in which you are required to have self-control and list the positive reasons for those limitations.

2. Consider a car driving down the wrong side of the road. A plane that veers off its flight plan. A cyclist who refuses to stay in the bike lane. A ship that ignores the warning of the lighthouse. Restrictions are meant to create a safer environment. Imagine the consequences of being an adult man who has not learned the value of self-control. Where could the lack of self-control lead?

3. How can you lead by example those you influence by your self-control? Right now, how can you challenge your buddies to join you on this quest to be a godly man of self-control? What can you do to keep each other accountable?

Historical Figure

Chose a person from history (past or present) whom you feel exhibits the qualities of self-control. You may choose from the list provided in the resource guide in Part Four of this book or select one of your own. Do some research on this person (internet search, library books) and answer the following questions:

1. Why did you choose this individual?

2. What aspect of self-control do they exhibit?

3. Explain how they lived this out in their daily life.

4. What did they have to sacrifice, if anything, to be self-controlled?

Biography/Autobiography

If you like to read, select a biography or autobiography on this individual to read throughout this month. Your parent may ask you to provide a book report or synopsis (personal choice for format) on what you read, paying special attention to your subject's self-control.

## Media Option

Is there a movie or documentary on the historical figure you chose? If so, take some time to watch it and write down several things you can identity about their life of self-control.

 ## Mentoring

Choose a mentor who exhibits qualities of self-control you or your parents admire. Maybe you know someone with lots of money, but rather than spending all of it on themselves they choose to help others first. Do you know someone who loves sweet treats but understands the harm eating it can do so chooses to eat healthier versions instead? Get together (how often is up to you, but often one meeting is sufficient as there are many other mentors involved in this process) and listen as they share their life experiences with you. Your parents will help guide the content of your discussions along with your mentor's ideas. If your mentor provides charts, lists, or diagrams as visuals, insert them into your binder for this chapter, along with any notes you may take. Possible discussion questions may include:
- An area of self-control that I work hard at is…
- An area where I lack self-control is…
- Reasons why I stay committed to self-control in this area is because…
- The role prayer plays in my pursuit of self-control is…

 # Journal Page

1. What, if anything, did the Lord imprint on your heart during your study of self-control?

2. Are there things about this study that bother you or you do not agree with? Explain.

3. If you worked on an area where you lacked self-control this month do you think you could continue to pursue it moving forward? Why or why not?

4. Spend some time in prayer asking the Lord to continue to build in you the desire to have self-control and not give in to the immediate desires of your flesh.

5. Review your memory verse.

Alternative Learning Pages
Do all or some of the following 7 activities

Activity 1 - If you like to be imaginative and creative, come up with a board game where there are consequences for self-indulgence (lose a turn, go back 3 spaces, get stuck in a swamp, etc.) and rewards for self-control (move ahead 4 spaces, jump to a certain square, collect coins, etc.). Feel free to use color, include playing pieces, coins for positive choices, or instruction cards. This will take a while to complete and make playable so this may be the only activity completed in this lesson. When you have made the game take a picture of it and insert it into your binder for this chapter. Invite family and friends to play along with you.

Activity 2 – Read, or have someone read for you, the biblical figure studies for both the godly trait and pitfall in the first section of this chapter. Make a list comparing the self-controlled actions versus the self-indulgent actions of the characters. Is there a theme you can see for each? Write one sentence summarizing what you observe.

Self-Controlled actions	Self-Indulgent actions
Summary	Summary

Activity 3 – In what areas of your life do you exhibit self-control? Make a list on the lines in the first column below. In what areas are you self-indulgent or lacking self-control? Use the second column to record your answers. Think of one way you can work on having more self-control for each of the areas you list. For this whole month work on these areas then record the results at the end of the month. Pray and ask God to help you in that effort.

Self-Control	Self-Indulgent
_____	_____
_____	_____
_____	_____
_____	_____

Ways I Can Work on Self-Control

_____

_____

_____

Results

_____

Activity 4 – If you like to draw and color, draw a picture of Nehemiah building the wall. Your scene can include anything from the account in Nehemiah 4. Color it and place it in your binder for this chapter.

Activity 5 – Write, or have someone write for you, a story. Include a scenario where someone chooses to have either self-control or to indulge themselves. Include two different endings. Conclude with a statement about which ending you feel was best and which one would have been the easiest. Write your story on a separate piece of paper and insert it into your binder for this chapter.

Activity 6 – Fill in the blanks with words from the word bank

- _____ vowed not to harm the King.

- Self-control means you sacrifice _____ now for a greater purpose.

- The secret to his strength, _____, was given up for the love of a woman.

- Both Nehemiah and Daniel _____, asking God to help them in their difficult situations.

- _____ and _____ disobeyed and let their desire for knowledge cloud their thinking.

- Another word for self-control is _____.

- David's _____ desires had dire consequences.

- Nehemiah's job was to _____ the wall.

- Daniel chose to eat _____ instead of the _____.

- The Jews who built the wall did their _____ with one hand and held their _____ in another.

Adam	gratification	rebuild	work	restraint
King's food	prayed	not cutting his hair	Daniel	
spear	vegetables	Eve	fleshly	

Activity 7 – Choose one of the verses from the Scripture study and try to memorize it. If memorizing is hard, put it to music, make up a poem, or draw a picture to illustrate it.

Chapter Eight

Humility vs. Pride

MONTHLY PLANNING PAGE

MONTH _____   CHARACTER TRAIT _____   PITFALL _____

HOMEWORK SECTION   COMPLETED
(insert on each line below the homework sections you will complete for this trait)

WEEK 1

MENTOR _____

DATES WE MEET _____

☐ ☐ ☐ ☐

_____

MEMORY VERSE _____

HISTORICAL FIGURE _____

WEEK 2

☐ ☐ ☐ ☐

BIOGRAPHY/AUTOBIOGRAPGY TITLE (if applicable) _____

SEXUAL PURIITY STUDY GUIDE TITLE (if applicable) _____

WEEK 3

☐ ☐ ☐ ☐

SERVICE PROJECTS (if applicable) _____

_____

_____

WEEK 4

☐ ☐ ☐ ☐

DATES PROJECTS COMPLETED _____

_____

NOTES, PAPERS, RESEARCH INSERTED IN BINDER:

YES   NO

Godly Trait – Humility

In his article, "The Awful Sin of Pride," David Wilkerson says, "Humility is total dependency on God. It is trusting God to do the right thing at the right time in the right way. It is trusting him to use you in the right way at the right time. Humility is patiently waiting on the Lord in a spirit of expectant faith." [9]

Another facet of humility acknowledges that the things we are good at, our talents and abilities, come from the Lord and are not ours to brag about or criticize. Humility puts others first and recognizes what they can contribute. A humble person admits their mistakes and failures rather than deflecting or making excuses. Humility shows up when we can admit we do not know everything and are willing to be teachable. A humble person does not need recognition and takes joy in the successes of others. The Bible has a lot to say about the value of being humble. It is important to God, so it needs to be important to us.

 **Scripture Study**

Psalm 25:9
He guides the humble in what is right and teaches them his way.

Psalm 149:4
For the LORD takes delight in his people; he crowns the humble with victory.

Proverbs 22:4
Humility is the fear of the LORD; its wages are riches and honor and life.

Philippians 2:3
Do nothing out of selfish ambition or vain conceit. Rather, in humility value others above yourselves.

James 4:10
Humble yourselves before the Lord, and he will lift you up.

Biblical Figure Study

Jesus – Philippians 2:6-8
Who, being in very nature God, did not consider equality with God something to be used to his own advantage; rather, he made himself nothing by taking the very nature of a servant, being made in human likeness. And being found in appearance as a man, he humbled himself by becoming obedient to death – even death on a cross!

No example in Scripture comes close to Jesus, showing us what a humble person looks like. Not only did he become a human baby, but he also humbled himself to be crucified on a cross, rather than to be exalted as a king.

John the Baptist – John 1:26-31
Now this was John's testimony when the Jewish leaders in Jerusalem sent priests and Levites to ask him who he was. He did not fail to confess, but confessed freely, "I am not the Messiah." They asked him, "Then who are you? Are you Elijah?" He said, "I am not." "Are you the Prophet?" He answered, "No." Finally they said, "Who are you? Give us an answer to take back to those who sent us. What do you say about yourself?" John replied in the words of Isaiah the prophet, "I am the voice of one calling in the wilderness, 'Make straight the way for the Lord.'" Now the Pharisees who had been sent questioned him, "Why then do you baptize if you are not the Messiah, nor Elijah, nor the Prophet?" "I baptize with water," John replied, "but among you stands one you do not know. He is the one who comes after me, the straps of whose sandals I am not worthy to untie."

John's only purpose in life was to proclaim the coming of Jesus the Messiah, preaching and baptizing. He garnered a following of disciples as he preached from place to place. He never took credit for his following and knew that Jesus was the main attraction, he was simply the opening act!

King Nebuchadnezzar - Read Daniel 4:27-37

You may wonder why this guy is listed as an example for humility. He could also be listed under pride, and indeed he is an example of both. He had great pride and arrogance about his wealth and vast kingdom. He thought he was all that and then some. But Daniel interpreted a dream for the King telling him he needs to acknowledge that all he has comes from God or it will be taken away from him. Nebuchadnezzar, after a time of humiliation and great loss, does acknowledge the might of God and worships him.

Pitfall – Pride

The Bible repeatedly speaks against pride. Pride dishonors the Lord, and he speaks harshly about the proud. Pride, at its root, can bring about the downfall of the heart. Pride can lead to deception, anger, bitterness, and unforgiveness. A prideful person thinks more of himself than he should. He is self-centered and arrogant. A prideful heart refuses to admit mistakes and accuses others of the wrongdoing. It is hard to forgive and accept forgiveness if you harbor pride in your heart. It can be difficult to admit you are wrong and easy to believe the other person does not deserve your forgiveness.

In the same article referenced above from David Wilkerson, he shares a fresh perspective and a broader definition of pride. "Pride is independence—humility is dependence. Pride is an unwillingness to wait for God to act in his own time and in his own way. Pride rushes in to take matters into its own hands. One of the greatest temptations true Christians face is getting ahead of God. It is acting without a clear mandate from God. It is taking things into our own hands when it appears that God is not working fast enough. It is impatience." (10)

Scripture Study

Isaiah 2:11
The eyes of the arrogant will be humbled and human pride brought low; the LORD alone will be exalted in that day.

Psalm 10:4
In his pride the wicked man does not seek him; in all his thoughts there is no room for God.

Proverbs 8:13
To fear the LORD is to hate evil; I hate pride and arrogance, evil behavior and perverse speech.

Proverbs 13:10
Where there is strife, there is pride, but wisdom is found in those who take advice.

1 John 2:16
For everything in the world—the lust of the flesh, the lust of the eyes, and the pride of life—comes not from the Father, but from the world.

Biblical Figure Study

King Saul – 1 Samuel 13:7-14
Saul remained at Gilgal, and all the troops with him were quaking with fear. He waited seven days, the time set by Samuel; but Samuel did not come to Gilgal, and Saul's men began to scatter. So he said,

"Bring me the burnt offering and the fellowship offerings." And Saul offered up the burnt offering. Just as he finished making the offering, Samuel arrived, and Saul went out to greet him. "What have you done?" asked Samuel. Saul replied, "When I saw that the men were scattering, and that you did not come at the set time, and that the Philistines were assembling at Mikmash, I thought, 'Now the Philistines will come down against me at Gilgal, and I have not sought the LORD's favor.' So I felt compelled to offer the burnt offering." "You have done a foolish thing," Samuel said. "You have not kept the command the LORD your God gave you; if you had, he would have established your kingdom over Israel for all time. But now your kingdom will not endure; the LORD has sought out a man after his own heart and appointed him ruler of his people, because you have not kept the LORD's command."

Only the priest could offer the sacrifice. Saul grew impatient waiting for Samuel, who was a prophet and a priest, so Saul did the sacrifice himself. Rather than trusting in God's promise and the word of Samuel, he took matters into his own hands. The result was the destruction of his kingdom. Saul's impatient pride got him into trouble.

<u>King Nebuchadnezzar</u> – reference his story again in Daniel 4. Nebuchadnezzar's pride cost him a great deal. He gloated about his wealth and position. See how God humbled him!

Humility vs. Pride Homework

1. List several ways pride can manifest itself (use the trait/pitfall descriptions and any Scripture references as hints).

2. Do you struggle with any of the prideful areas you listed? Explain your answer and list some examples.

3. In the story of John the Baptist, think of ways John might have practiced humility in order to prevent pride from getting a foothold.

4. The story referenced here about King Nebuchadnezzar shows God's amazing grace in taking a soul burdened with pride and transforming it to praise, offering forgiveness. Was there a time in your life when you struggled with pride in a certain area (a musical/physical talent, academic knowledge, etc.) that God had to humble you in a difficult way because you did not seek humility? Share your experience? Was it embarrassing, painful? What did you learn as a result?

5. King Saul's pride, in the passage above, manifested itself through his impatience. When he got caught by Samuel what was Saul's response? Did he humble himself and repent?

6. Share a time when you humbly admitted a mistake, or a wrongdoing, showed humility in needing to ask for help or accepted the consequences of a poor choice with humility. What kind of reaction did you get from the other person?

7. Read the following article on Pride vs. Humility. You may want to spend one day on each trait as the sections are long. Write down (or print the article and use a highlighter) anything new you learn about each, or points you want to remember. When completed, put your notes in your binder for this chapter. https://tinyurl.com/xtry5unx [11]

8. Choose a scripture from the verses above on humility and commit it to memory. Reference your choice here and record it on your monthly planning page.

Becoming a Woman of Humility

Hey gals, the following questions are just for you. Take the time to work through them, being as honest as you can.

1. The pitfall of humility is arrogance or pride. What does a prideful woman look like? What natural gifts has the Lord given women that can become areas of pride? Think of the adult women in your life and the good qualities they possess. What are the outcomes if pride takes a foothold in those areas?

2. Look at Philippians 2:3 from the Scripture study for humility. Insert your name in the blanks. (_____), "Do nothing out of selfish ambition or vain conceit. Rather, (_____), in humility value others above yourselves."

How does this verse directly impact you? What do you do out of selfish ambition? What about vain conceit? Look that up if you are unfamiliar with the term. How can you value others above yourself?

3. What is attractive about a young lady who is humble (I am not referring to physical attraction but rather her influence or impact)? Ask your dad or an older brother or another adult male. What draws them to humility? Is this something you would like to pursue? Why or why not?

Becoming a Man of Humility

Hey guys, the following questions are just for you. Take the time to work through them, being as honest as you can.

1. The pitfall of humility is arrogance or pride. What does a prideful man look like? What natural gifts has the Lord given men that can become areas of pride? Think of the adult men in your life and the good qualities they possess. What are the outcomes if pride takes a foothold in those areas?

2. Look at Psalm 10:4 from the Scripture study for pride. *"In his pride the wicked man does not seek him; in all his thoughts there is no room for God."* Why would there be no room for God? What are possible dangers for a man's heart if pride takes a foothold?

3. Men can possess many great qualities. Maybe you can debug technical problems, or you have a quick mind to see various potential solutions, the ability to make logical decisions based on facts, or maybe you easily recognize needs and jump in to help. With so many great qualities, and many more not listed, becoming self-reliant on your strengths could be easy to do. How can you resist the temptation to rely on self and humbly depend on the Lord? Does Psalm 25:9 help? "He guides the humble in what is right and teaches them his way."

Historical Figure

Choose a person from history (past or present) whom you feel exhibits qualities of humility. You may choose from the list provided in the resource guide, Part Four, or select one of your own. Do some research on this person (internet search, library books) and answer the following questions:

1. Why did you choose this individual?

2. What aspect of humility do they exhibit?

3. Explain how they lived this out in their daily life.

4. What were the outcomes of their choosing humility over pride? Did they have to sacrifice anything to be humble?

5. Did they show moments of pride? Explain

_____

_____

Biography/Autobiography

If you like to read, select a biography or autobiography on this individual to read throughout this month. Your parent may ask you to provide a book report or synopsis (personal choice for format) on what you read, paying special attention to your subject's humility.

 # Media Option

Is there a movie or documentary on the historical person you chose? If so, take some time to watch it and write down several things you can identify about their life of humility.

 # Mentoring

Choose a mentor who exhibits qualities of humility you or your parents admire. Is there someone who has lived a simple life, or someone who always gives others credit, or maybe someone who asks more questions of others than speaking about themselves? Alternatively, you may know someone who has struggled with the sin of pride and has had to be humbled as a result. Get together (how often is up to you, but often one meeting is sufficient as there are many other mentors involved in this process) and listen as they share their life experiences with you. Your parent(s) will help guide the content of your discussions along with your mentor's ideas. If your mentor provides charts, lists, or diagrams as visuals, insert them into your binder for this chapter, along with any notes you may take. Possible discussion questions may include:
- I have struggled with pride in my life in these ways…
- The consequences of my pride were…
- Ways I practice humility are…

Journal Page

1. What, if anything, did the Lord imprint on your heart during your study of humility?

2. What are your thoughts about the things your mentor shared when they faced challenges with pride?

3. Are there areas of pride in your own life that need to be addressed? How can you begin to practice humility in these areas?

4. Spend some time talking with Jesus. Tell him about where you struggle, confess your pride, and seek his forgiveness. Ask the Lord to create a humble spirit in you.

5. Review the memory verse.

Alternative Learning Page
Do all or some of the following 8 activities

Activity 1 – Read, or have someone read for you, the Scripture studies at the beginning of this chapter on humility and pride. Make a list of words that describe how a humble person might be different than a proud person.

Humble	Pride
_____	_____
_____	_____
_____	_____
_____	_____
_____	_____

Activity 2 – Look at the Bible verses that talk about the humility of Jesus. Draw a picture, write a poem, find a way to express how you see that passage in a real scene. Use a separate piece of paper and insert into the folder at the back of the chapter.

Activity 3 – Reference the passage on John the Baptist. Imagine you were him and your purpose was to preach about the coming Messiah and challenge people to repent.

1. What would you think of your "job"?
2. Would that be easy or difficult?
3. If you were baptizing people in the river and Jesus walked up to you asking to be baptized, what would you say?
4. Do you think you would have any jealousy when Jesus's crowds and his followers grew bigger than yours and your followers started to leave and follow Jesus?

Sit in those feelings for a bit and write down, or dictate to a parent, how that feels.

_____
_____
_____
_____

Activity 4 – Think of a time you felt pride in your heart because you are good at something (skateboard jumps, parkour, playing piano, singing, art, 3-point shots).

1. After studying the scriptures referenced above about humility and pride, how do you think God wants you to respond to the things you do well?

   _____

2. What will happen to your heart if you let pride settle and go unchecked and unrepented?

   _____

3. Take a minute to pray and confess your sin of pride and ask Jesus to help you be humble and more thankful for the talents you have.

Activity 5 – Match the words to humility or pride.

John the Baptist		King Saul
Repentance		Worship
Excuses	Pride	Independence
Impatience		Expectant faith
Dependence		Pride of life
Advice	Humility	Strife
Others first		Teachable
Arrogance		Always right

Activity 6 – If you like building with colored blocks, select several red pieces and several white pieces. With red representing pride and white representing humility, build a character or scene from one of the Bible stories above to show those traits. Take a picture, print it, and insert it into your binder for this chapter.

Activity 7 - Fill in the blanks with words from the box to finish the sentences. Some words may be used more than once. Scripture references given offer clues to blanks.

- John the Baptist said he was not _____ to untie Jesus's sandals.

- King Saul got tired of _____ so went ahead and offered the sacrifice to God.

- King Nebuchadnezzar was very _____ and prideful. God brought him low by making him like an _____.

- But then King Nebuchadnezzar _____ and _____ and _____ God.

- Though equal to God, Jesus _____ himself by taking on the form of a man.

- God _____ the humble and _____ them his way.

- God says, "I hate _____ and _____".

- The _____ of the flesh, the _____ of the eyes, and the _____ of life comes not from the _____ but from the _____.

lust	guides	Psalm 25:9	world	worthy	Proverbs 8:13
rich	animal	humbled	pride	teaches	honored
waiting	Daniel 4:34	Father	arrogance	praised	glorified
John 2:16					

Activity 8 – Choose a Bible verse from the humility Scripture study and memorize it using music, rhyming, poetry, repetition, or movement. Share it with mom or dad.

Chapter Nine

Obedience vs. Disobedience

MONTHLY PLANNING PAGE

MONTH _____ CHARACTER TRAIT _____ PITFALL _____

HOMEWORK SECTION   **COMPLETED**   MENTOR _____
(insert on each line below the homework sections you will complete for this trait)

WEEK 1
_____   ☐ ☐ ☐ ☐   DATES WE MEET _____
_____   _____
_____   MEMORY VERSE _____
_____   HISTORICAL FIGURE _____

WEEK 2
_____   ☐ ☐ ☐ ☐   BIOGRAPHY/AUTOBIOGRAPGY TITLE (if applicable) _____
_____   _____
_____   SEXUAL PURITY STUDY GUIDE TITLE (if applicable) _____
_____   _____

WEEK 3
_____   ☐ ☐ ☐ ☐   SERVICE PROJECTS (if applicable) _____
_____   _____
_____   _____
_____   DATES PROJECTS COMPLETED _____

WEEK 4
_____   ☐ ☐ ☐ ☐   _____
_____   NOTES, PAPERS, RESEARCH INSERTED IN BINDER:
_____
_____   YES   NO

Godly Trait – Obedience

When you were little (and maybe you still do it) did you ever ask your parents "why" when they told you to do something? And did they ever give you the answer, "Because I said so"? As we get older, sometimes we need more than just a simple explanation for obedience. Sometimes obeying can get complicated and confusing. For example, can we stay in the will of God if we are disobedient to God? Or what if we do not understand why God is asking us to do something? Do we still obey? If you listen to Christian music, you are likely familiar with the artist Chris Tomlin. He has recorded a song called "I Will Follow" [12] Look it up on YouTube and listen to the lyrics. The YouTube link is listed in the endnotes of this book, citation #12. Following Jesus, living in obedience to him, requires that we do as he would do, and go where he would go. This is not an easy task. Let's dive into Scripture to see what God says about it.

 **Scripture Study**

1 Samuel 15:22
But Samuel replied: "Does the LORD delight in burnt offerings and sacrifices as much as in obeying the LORD? To obey is better than sacrifice, and to heed is better than the fat of rams.

Deuteronomy 5:33
Walk in obedience to all that the LORD your God has commanded you, so that you may live and prosper and prolong your days in the land that you will possess.

Psalm 119:34
Give me understanding, so that I may keep your law and obey it with all my heart.

2 John 1:6
And this is love: that we walk in obedience to his commands. As you have heard from the beginning, his command is that you walk in love.

Ephesians 6:1-3
Children, obey your parents in the Lord, for this is right. Honor your father and mother – which is the first commandment with a promise – so that it may go well with you and that you may enjoy long life on the earth.

Biblical Figure Study

<u>Mary the Mother of Jesus</u> – Read Luke 1:26-38, 46-56

Read the account of the angel appearing to Mary to explain how she would bear the son of God. A monumental ask on God's part, and to a young girl. Her faith and obedience to willingly walk into this role is astonishing.

<u>Abraham</u> – Genesis 12:1-4
The LORD had said to Abram, "Go from your country, your people and your father's household to the land I will show you. I will make you into a great nation, and I will bless you; I will make your name great, and you will be a blessing. I will bless those who bless you, and whoever curses you I will curse; and all peoples on earth will be blessed through you." So Abram went, as the LORD had told him; and Lot went with him. Abram was seventy-five years old when he set out from Harran. He took his wife Sarai, his nephew Lot, all the possessions they had accumulated and the people they had acquired in Harran, and they set out for the land of Canaan, and they arrived there.

Being told to "go" but not told where—that is risky at best. Yet he obeyed the call of God on his life and went, listening all the way to God's voice.

Pitfall – Disobedience

Dictionary.com defines disobedience as "failure or refusal to obey rules or someone in authority." [13]

Jerry Bridges, author of *The Pursuit of Holiness*, notes, "The Christian living in disobedience also lives devoid of joy and hope. But when he begins to understand that Christ has delivered him from the reign of sin, when he begins to see that he is united to him who has all power and authority and that it is possible to walk in obedience, he begins to have hope, and as he hopes in Christ, he begins to have joy. In the strength of this joy, he begins to overcome the sins that have so easily entangle him. He then finds that the joy of a holy walk is infinitely more satisfying than the fleeting pleasures of sin. But to experience this joy, we must make some choices. We must choose to forsake sin, not only because it is defeating to us but because it grieves the heart of God." [14]

# Scripture Study

<u>Jeremiah 7:28</u>
Therefore say to them, 'This is the nation that has not obeyed the LORD its God or responded to correction. Truth has perished; it has vanished from their lips.

<u>Deuteronomy 28:15</u>
However, if you do not obey the LORD your God and do not carefully follow all his commands and decrees I am giving you today, all these curses will come on you and overtake you:

<u>1 Samuel 12:15</u>
But if you do not obey the LORD, and if you rebel against his commands, his hand will be against you, as it was against your ancestors.

<u>Romans 5:19</u>
For just as through the disobedience of the one man the many were made sinners, so also through the obedience of the one man the many will be made righteous.

# Biblical Figure Study

<u>Moses</u> – Read Number 20:1-12

The consequences of Moses' choice were devastating. They could have been so easily avoided and really, what God had asked him to do was rather simple. Yet he felt changing the instructions and doing it his way was better. It was a poor choice.

<u>Jonah</u> – Read Jonah 1:1-17

Poor Jonah. He allowed fear to turn into cowardice. His resulting disobedience led him to be swallowed by a fish. Because God had a specific job for him, he was still required to do it, so he went through all the turmoil unnecessarily.

 **Obedience vs. Disobedience Homework**

1. As you read the Scripture passage about Mary, the mother of Jesus, if you are a girl, put yourself in her shoes. If you are a guy, imagine you are Joseph. If you are not familiar with the story, Joseph and Mary were engaged to be married. Joseph also had an angel appear to him. If an angel appeared telling you not to be afraid, then shared this life-altering news, what would be your first reaction?

2. Compare your reaction to Mary's from the above passage or Joseph's from Matthew 1:18-24. What does Mary say and how does her obedience play out? If you are envisioning being Joseph, what would that be like?

3. Read this passage in Luke 1 in various translations, if you can. (The You Version Bible app downloaded from an app store on any smart phone allows you to select a passage in any version you like. Versions are the same Bible written in different languages and language styles, from traditional to contemporary, and from formal to conversational. You can also Google different translations for different readings). Write down the words Mary uses and notice any difference in phrases. Do some translations provide a better understanding for you than others?

4. In the story about Moses, how do you feel about the consequence God handed him? Did the punishment fit the crime so to speak? Do you feel it was justified or unwarranted? Explain your answer.

5. In which areas of your life do you struggle to be obedient? Be honest. Why is it so hard to obey sometimes?

6. Like Jonah, has God ever brought you to a place of obedience, kicking and screaming, where you ended up surrendering your will and obeying?

7. Like Abraham, have you obeyed your parents' wishes (or God's) without knowing all the details or how it will turn out? If yes, what was that process like? Is it hard to obey when you do not see how it will turn out?

8. Choose one of the verses on obedience and commit it to memory. Reference the verse you chose here and record it on your monthly planning page.

Becoming a Woman of Obedience

Hey gals, the following questions are just for you. Take some time to work through them, and be as honest as you can.

1. As you grow into womanhood, the concept of obedience may feel unfair to you. As a young girl it makes sense to obey your parents, teachers, or others in authority over you. But when you are an adult, it may not feel right to be expected to "obey." Should you obey a husband? Other adults? Try to imagine being a wife and mom down the road or an adult woman who is self-sufficient, living on her own. How does obedience play out as a grown up in your mind? Do the verses about obedience in the Bible only apply to kids? What about 1 Corinthians 11:3?

2. There is a predominant movement in today's culture that conveys a message to girls that you do not need anybody, you can do what you want, no one can tell you what to do. While girls should understand that they are whole and complete the way they are and do not need a man to fulfill them or give them worth, the cultural tone sends the wrong kind of message to young girls. Based on the scriptures listed above in the Scripture study, how does godly obedience for you as a young lady stand in contrast to what the world screams at you?

3. As a girl, do you feel obedience makes you appear inferior or inequal? Can you be fully submissive and yet strong and bold and assertive? Are there any scriptures that can guide your answer?

Do not give in to the notion that because you desire to honor God by living obediently before him you are giving up your free will, or that your goals and dreams are stifled if you are submissive to God or others. Pursue your passions, seek to find your purpose, chase after your dreams. You can be strong and confident while submitting to the will of your Father who wants nothing but good things for you.

Becoming a Man of Obedience

Hey guys, the following questions are just for you. Take some time to work through them, and be as honest as you can.

1. The goal of this entire study is to learn and experience the various character qualities that will help you become a godly man. Obedience may be a hard one when it comes to imagining how that plays out as a grown man, possibly with a wife and children someday. We spend a lot of time talking about obeying parents and teachers, but when you are an adult what do you think obedience would look like?

2. If the Lord blesses you with a family, one of your roles in your family will be to lead them spiritually. 1 Corinthians 11:3 says, "But I want you to realize that the head of every man is Christ, and the head of the woman is man, and the head of Christ is God." Ephesians 5:25 says, "Husbands, love your wives, just as Christ loved the church and gave himself up for her." Using your answer(s) to question 1, how do you lead by example in teaching your family obedience to the Lord? Think through things like tithing, church attendance, serving, etc.

3. Obedience requires a submissive heart. Sometimes for guys who want to be strong and in charge, it feels like the opposite to be submissive. Do you feel like it is a sign of weakness, with your friends, to surrender your will to those in authority over you? How can you be a strong leader and be obedient and submissive to the Lord at the same time?

Society sends the message to guys today that you should be in complete control. Submitting is a sign of weakness; not standing up to authority makes you soft. There are situations as a Christian man when standing up against evil, injustice and anything that goes against Scripture is required. But do not be fooled into thinking that your obedience to the Lord, surrendering your will and submitting to those in authority over you, is weak. Rather, it shows a strength of character and a pursuit of godliness. Go for it, guys!

Historical Figure

Choose a person from history (past or present) who you feel exhibits qualities of obedience. You may choose from the list provided in the resource guide, Part Four, or select one of your own. Do some research on this person (internet search, library books) and answer the following questions:

1. Why did you choose this individual?

2. What aspect of obedience do they exhibit?

3. Explain how they lived this out in their daily lives.

4. What obstacles, if any, did they have to overcome to live a life of obedience?

5. Were there any moments when they chose disobedience instead? Explain.

Biography/Autobiography

If you like to read, select a biography or autobiography on this individual to read throughout this month. Your parent may ask you to provide a book report or synopsis (personal choice for format) on what you read, paying special attention to your subject's commitment to obedience.

 # Media Option

Is there a movie or documentary on the historic person you chose? If so, take some time to watch it and write down several things you can identify about their life of obedience.

 # Mentoring

Choose a mentor who exhibits qualities of obedience that you or your parents admire. Maybe find someone who has followed God into an unknown future, was called to move far away to do ministry, or always thought they would be or do something specific, but God directed them otherwise. Get together (how often is up to your mentor and parent, but often one meeting is sufficient as there are many other mentors involved in this process) and listen as they share their life experiences with you. Your parents will help guide the content of your discussions along with your mentor's ideas. If your mentor provides charts, lists, or diagrams as visuals, insert them into your binder for this chapter, along with any notes you may take. Possible discussion questions may include:
- Sometimes being obedient is hard because…
- There have been times I was not obedient. I went my own way because…
- The result was …
- Blessings I have received from being obedient to the Lord are…

Journal Page

1. What, if anything, did the Lord imprint on your heart during your study of obedience?

2. Are there areas of disobedience you need to confess to God? Write them down.

3. Do you need to confess these areas to your parents and make anything right with them?

4. Spend some time talking to God, confessing your sin, and receiving his forgiveness and encouragement.

5. Review your memory verse.

Alternative Learning Pages
Do all or some of the following 8 activities

Activity 1 – Read, or have someone read for you, the Scripture study sections for both Obedience and Disobedience at the beginning of this chapter. Write on the lines below, or share with someone, any common themes you see referenced for each trait.

_____

_____

_____

Activity 2 – Read, or have someone read for you, the biblical figure study sections for both Obedience and Disobedience. Fill in the chart below comparing actions/behaviors of the obedient to the actions/behaviors of the disobedient. Include the consequences for the disobedient choice and blessings for the obedient choice. You may need to infer if the answer is not explicitly in Scripture.

	Actions/Behaviors	Consequences	Blessings
Obedient			
Disobedient			

Activity - 3 – Think over the last couple of weeks. What things have your mom or dad, or a schoolteacher, asked you to do that you did not obey?

1. Write down a few things on the lines below.

_____

_____

_____

2. It is possible that your parents or teacher did not know you were disobedient. If that is the case, write down how you felt getting away with something you should not have. If you prefer to draw a picture than to write, feel free to draw on a separate sheet of paper. Insert it into your binder for this chapter.

Activity 4 – Music can be a powerful influence for young people these days. Not all music conveys positive God-honoring messages. Some artists criticize authority and encourage rebellion. With your parents' permission and/or supervision, do a Google search and see if you can find a song or two that fits what is described here. Listen carefully to the lyrics and write down, or share with your parent, what the messages are that are being conveyed. Do either of them speak about honoring and obeying those in authority over you? What can happen when we fill our minds with negative messages?

Activity 5 – In the story of Jonah in 1:1-17, put yourself in his shoes. Imagine that you have been asked by your school principal to sit with a new student at lunch. You are to befriend them, ask questions, and offer to show them around campus. This new student, however, is not nice and seems to bully everyone who tries to be kind. You have seen them push kids in the hall, pretend to listen in class while playing on their phone, and laugh at other kids who get answers wrong. The last thing you want to do is be their friend let alone spend your lunch hour sitting with them. You talk to your principal and give all sorts of reasons why you cannot do what he is asking. You explain that you think this student is mean and would be better off just sitting by themselves. You mention you are surprised he could attend the school given his bully nature and his disrespect for rules and authority. The principal tells you he is aware of these things, but you still need to help him out. Think about how this would make you feel? Would you have some anxiety? Think about the people Jonah was told to preach to? Why do you think God asks us to do things that are so hard sometimes? Write or have a parent write your answers for you.

Activity 6 – Fill in the blanks with words from the word bank

1. Moses _____ the _____ instead of speaking to it.
2. Abraham obeyed and _____ the Lord wherever he was led.
3. Mary was _____ by the Lord.
4. Mary's response to the angel's announcement was, "May your _____ to me be _____".
5. All the people on Earth would be _____ through Abraham.
6. Moses did not trust God enough to _____ Him before the _____ community.

Highly
Favored
Israelite
Blessed
Rock
Followed
Honor
Fulfilled
Struck
Word

Activity 7 – At the beginning of the chapter there is a quote by Pastor Jerry Bridges. If you like to draw, on a separate piece of blank paper, illustrate this quote as you understand it. Insert it into your binder for this chapter.

Activity 8 – Choose a verse from one of the Scripture studies above for either obedience or disobedience. Write out each word on a note card. Arrange them in proper order then read the verse. After each recitation remove one word until you can recite the verse from memory.

Chapter Ten

Wisdom vs. Foolishness

MONTHLY PLANNING PAGE

MONTH _____ CHARACTER TRAIT _____ PITFALL _____

HOMEWORK SECTION COMPLETED MENTOR _____
(insert on each line below the homework sections you will complete for this trait)

WEEK 1
☐ ☐ ☐ ☐ DATES WE MEET _____
_____
_____ MEMORY VERSE _____
_____ HISTORICAL FIGURE _____

WEEK 2
☐ ☐ ☐ ☐ BIOGRAPHY/AUTOBIOGRAPHY TITLE (if applicable) _____
_____
_____ SEXUAL PURITY STUDY GUIDE TITLE (if applicable) _____
_____

WEEK 3
☐ ☐ ☐ ☐ SERVICE PROJECTS (if applicable) _____
_____
_____
_____

WEEK 4
☐ ☐ ☐ ☐ DATES PROJECTS COMPLETED _____
_____
_____ NOTES, PAPERS, RESEARCH INSERTED IN BINDER:
_____   YES   NO

Godly Trait – Wisdom

Pastor and author Timothy Keller wrote, "Proverbs chapter 4 is filled with the repeated exhortation 'do not forsake' wisdom. The message is clear: Never, ever give up in your pursuit of wisdom. Do absolutely anything to get it, whatever it costs you. Why? Because it is more costly to not have it. You will make decisions that lead to one difficulty and disaster after another. So do whatever it takes." (15)

 ## Scripture Study

Psalm 37:30
The mouths of the righteous utter wisdom, and their tongues speak what is just.

Proverbs 1:1-7
The proverbs of Solomon son of David, king of Israel: for gaining wisdom and instruction; for understanding words of insight; for receiving instruction in prudent behavior, doing what is right and just and fair; for giving prudence to those who are simple, knowledge and discretion to the young – let the wise listen and add to their learning, and let the discerning get guidance – for understanding proverbs and parables, the sayings and riddles of the wise. The fear of the LORD is the beginning of knowledge, but fools despise wisdom and instruction.

Proverbs 2 (the whole chapter)

Proverbs 4:7
The beginning of wisdom is this: Get wisdom. Though it cost all you have, get understanding.

Ephesians 1:17
I keep asking that the God of our Lord Jesus Christ, the glorious Father, may give you the Spirit of wisdom and revelation, so that you may know him better.

James 1:15
If any of you lacks wisdom, you should ask God, who gives generously to all without finding fault, and it will be given to you.

# Biblical Figure Study

<u>King Solomon</u> – Read 1 Kings 3:5-14

Of all the things a king could ask for he wanted wisdom and discernment. Notice God's response to his request.

<u>The Wise Builder</u> – Matthew 7:24-27
Therefore, everyone who hears these words of mine and puts them into practice is like a wise man who built his house on the rock. The rain came down, the streams rose, and the winds blew and beat against that house; yet it did not fall, because it had its foundation on the rock. But everyone who hears these words of mine and does not put them into practice is like a foolish man who built his house on sand. The rain came down, the streams rose, and the winds blew and beat against that house, and it fell with a great crash."

The wisdom to understand that a solid, strong foundation is crucial in building a house is a metaphor for how we are to build a strong foundation for our life.

Pitfall – Foolishness

In Tim Keller's book mentioned above, he addresses foolishness as the opposite of wisdom. He says, "Fools are people so habitually out of touch with reality that they make life miserable for themselves and all around them." He goes on, "But the ultimate foolishness is to make anything the center of our lives besides God. That will always lead to disappointment and breakdown. Fools fail to see [the] boundaries embedded in reality – physical, psychological, relational, and spiritual. They step outside them and wonder why they sink." (16)

# Scripture Study

<u>1 Samuel 13:13</u>
"You have done a foolish thing," Samuel said. "You have not kept the command the LORD your God gave you; if you had, he would have established your kingdom over Israel for all time.

Job 5:2
"You have done a foolish thing," Samuel said. "You have not kept the command the LORD your God gave you; if you had, he would have established your kingdom over Israel for all time.

Psalm 1:1.
Blessed is the one who does not walk in step with the wicked or stand in the way that sinners take or sit in the company of mockers

Psalm 107:17
Some became fools through their rebellious ways and suffered affliction because of their iniquities.

Proverbs 10:1, 8
A wise son brings joy to his father, but a foolish son brings grief to his mother. The wise in heart accept commands, but a chattering fool comes to ruin.

Ephesians 5:4
Nor should there be obscenity, foolish talk or coarse joking, which are out of place, but rather thanksgiving.

Biblical Figure Study

Asa – King of Judah – Read 2 Chronicles 14-16

Notice how King Asa's reign, up until the last few years, was God-honoring and obedient. Pay close attention to the choice he made in chapter 16 and how his life ends in the last few verses of that chapter. Fascinating!

The Israelites – Read Exodus 32

Oh, how often we act like the Israelites. One minute we are worshiping God for all He has done for us then the next we are whining and complaining because life is so hard. Read about how foolish they were when they got impatient waiting for Moses to come down from the mountain where he was talking to God.

Wisdom vs. Foolishness Homework

1. Look back at the character study of King Solomon. What were some of the things he could have asked God for, given his position? What does his request for wisdom reveal about his character?

2. In the parable of the wise builder, what made him wise in this scenario? What difference did it make in the outcome?

3. King Asa started out on a good footing then fell off the rails. In 2 Chronicles 16 read what he did. What was the consequence?

4. What were the reasons for the Israelites building the golden calf? What made this a foolish decision?

5. Think of a time you showed wisdom in a decision you made. Explain it here. What would the foolish choice have been and why did you not make that decision?

6. Conversely, think of a time you acted foolishly. Explain it here. What were the circumstances and share the outcome?

7. a. Think about some of the bigger life choices you will need to make as you become an adult. Write down 5 or 6.

   b. Choose 3 of those choices and think about the potential outcomes if you choose foolishly.

   c. Why is learning to make wise decisions now, when you are young, so important?

8. Choose a verse from the Scripture study on wisdom and commit it to memory. Reference it here and record it on your monthly planning page.

Becoming a Woman of Wisdom

Hey gals, the following questions are just for you. Take the time to work through them, being as honest as you can.

1. What do you think it means to chase after wisdom? Reference Proverbs 4:7. How are you chasing after wisdom, right now, in the decisions you face as a young lady?

2. Do not expect the man in your life, whether a boyfriend or husband, to be the only one responsible for pursuing wisdom. The Bible does not differentiate between men and women when it comes to getting wisdom. It is our responsibility to seek the Lord, pursue understanding, discernment, and wisdom. Read Proverbs 31:10-31. This passage is spoken of as "The Proverbs 31 Woman". Look at the list of all the things this woman does (this is a figurative woman). See how she possesses wisdom on her own. How does this passage empower you as a young woman to pursue these godly traits?

3. Judges 4 and 5 share the story of Deborah. She was a prophetess, Judge of Israel, and a songstress. Read her story and share a few ideas of how wisdom impacted the choices she made and what the results were. What take-aways are there for you in your present circumstances?

Resist the urge to run ahead on your own without first seeking wisdom from the Lord. If you have choices, it is possible the outcome of some of those choices would not be the best for you, a family or business. God gives us intelligence and the ability to think through decisions. Ask God for wisdom and that he will align your desires with his and his will for you.

Becoming a Man of Wisdom

1. What do you think it means to chase after wisdom? Reference Proverbs 4:7. How are you chasing after wisdom, right now, in the decisions you face as a young man?

2. Read Proverbs 2. Wow! What encouragement does this give you as a young man? Does understanding the fear of the Lord and finding the knowledge of God (v. 5) sound unattainable to you? What must you do to achieve it (vv. 1-4)? What does wisdom protect you from in vv. 9-22?

3. What decisions are you facing right now that need God's wisdom? Explain

Chase after wisdom, young man! Pursue it, be relentless about it. Seek to understand God and his ways so you can be the kind of man who, like King Solomon, finds great favor with God for desiring wisdom. Start while you are young.

 # Historical Figure

Choose a person (past or present) whom you feel exhibits qualities of wisdom. You may choose from the list provided in the resource guide in Part Four of this book or select one of your own. Do some research on the person (internet search, library books) and answer the following questions:

1. Why did you choose this individual?

2. What aspect of wisdom do they exhibit?

3. Explain how they lived this out in their daily life.

4. Do they have moments of foolishness? Explain.

Biography/Autobiography

If you like to read, select a biography or autobiography on this individual to read throughout this month. Your parent may ask you to provide a book report or synopsis (personal choice for format) on what you read, paying special attention to their commitment to chase after wisdom.

 # Media Option

Is there a movie or documentary on the historical person you chose? If so, take some time to watch it and write down several things you can identify about their life of wisdom.

 # Mentoring

Choose a mentor who exhibits qualities of wisdom that you or your parents admire. Get together (how often is up to you, but often one meeting is sufficient as there are many other mentors involved in this process) and listen as they share their life experiences with you. Your parent(s) will help guide the content of your discussions along with your mentor's ideas. If your mentor provides charts, lists, or diagrams as visuals, insert them into your binder for this chapter, along with any notes you may take. Possible discussion questions may include:

- How I worked on getting wisdom…
- Struggles with gaining wisdom…
- A time I chose the foolish over the wise decision…

Journal Page

1. What, if anything, did the Lord imprint on your heart during your study of wisdom?

2. Are there consistent areas of foolishness that you need to give up? Confess those.

3. How will you practice wisdom? What tools will you use to help?

4. Spend some time in prayer talking to God about what you have learned, including the lessons you learned from your mentor.

5. Review your memory verse.

Alternative Learning Pages
Do all or some of the following 8 activities

Activity 1 – Read or have someone read for you Proverbs 1:1-7. There are six phrases in the first half of the section that talk about what wisdom is for. Write them here or have someone write for you:

"The proverbs of Solomon son of David, king of Israel: for gaining wisdom and instruction; for understanding words of insight; for receiving instruction in prudent behavior, doing what is right and just and fair; for giving prudence to those who are simple, knowledge and discretion to the young – let the wise listen and add to their learning, and let the discerning get guidance – for understanding proverbs and parables, the sayings and riddles of the wise. The fear of the LORD is the beginning of knowledge, but fools despise wisdom and instruction".

1. Gaining _____ and _____.

2. Understanding _____ of _____

3. Receiving _____ in _____

4. Doing _____ is _____ and _____ and _____

5. Giving _____ to those who _____

6. Knowledge and _____ to the _____

Activity 2 – The wise builder in Matthew 7:24-27 is used to teach a lesson about wisdom. How is his choice considered a wise decision?

_____

_____

_____

Activity 3 – Who do you know who is wise? Interview them (over videoconference if they are not local) and ask the following questions? **PARENTS:** If your child is doing the mentoring portion of this program for this trait, these questions will likely be covered in those meetings so you can skip this question.

1. How did you become a wise person?
2. Have you made unwise choices? If so, can you give an example of what it was and how that turned out?

3. Give an example of a wise decision and the result?
4. Do you pray for wisdom?
5. What advice do you have for me when it comes to getting wisdom?

Activity 4 - Do the following word search puzzle, finding the words in the word bank

```
F U F H Q K C F Z I Y V A D I S A P P O I N T M E N T H V N
U K D O F H X L Q W X O I M C J I G V P D S M N S L U O E O
Y R Y Y V S T Q V Z L O H S U E A X J U U J W I L Z S O B D
M K R D P E L B R H A T F I N C H T M Z Y U T G J M H V Z J
Z Q E F C L K R G Z K O B S D H G H K R U Z U F V M H I Z C
M O H O Y S K S I K I B V R E H A O I N J T O O U N N I W I
S C I D Y L O N N S A E C J R Q P Q B K F Z B D H K S E S M
S A G E H C P L S Z M O C T S D Q K I I N T V D S K H L L M
G U I D A N C E T R J Z S A T H M P C I I N Q I O J F A B W
C R N I M U Y V R W W I C S A O D Z K V M C N L G K M N N J
H T R F E J B E U C S Z K B N T X K F T P G X U I P P M D U
H A F G E O R G C L D P Y T D O R P P Y U S Q N B F Z E V H
Q A B E F D J K T G E A G U I K G R F H L X T V I O O Z F J
O C R I G M Z V I G U I N L N B O U G C S U C U Q N Y P G G
U D G F W I S K O V W Y Y V G T J D G M I E D G H B Q N A P
W N R S J G W E N R W R G A I R N E Z E V K D G O P U D N P
U U I U A R U M E O M T W V L Q R N Z L E T I A C L U K I W
T O E Q P C T J S A W Z L W M F N C S O N U S F I C T K H V
N J F I G N O R A N T L G I S O P E P M E W C D O J B Q I R
D W T D W K E G U N L W E B S T C I X G S X R C K O B V W X
N E O H Z X J Y F L E I Z D U T T K V D S V E S Q G L I D S
J S C O N L H U P T A C O R G D E T E V Z T T J A X U I F N
B Q I E W N I E D G R K X A X E R N J R I T I E I T B E S P
B Q U S I B P V X A N E Z M C W V P N H S G O F J W D E A H
Q T B P S B F H B Z V D P L B F K M L P H P N P Y I H V L R
O J P Q E J L L J O W S G N R L E H C T P O O B O W E P O O
Q Y Q I J L D P B B F O X G T R S D L F X Q V Z T O B K W D
N M B E J X O X C S X J Z K V J Z K E V B Y Z F M B Y E X I
C Q L N M S H M A V F E G F B H G N S M U G Q M W D E W H I
X M F A Y P N K H D D M I M F G B M T W K P R F R N V F K B
```

wise	foolish	instruction	prudence	understanding
knowledge	learn	discretion	listen	guidance
grief	disappointment	impulsiveness	ignorant	

Activity 5 – If you like to write create a piece of writing that personifies the words Wisdom and Understanding as people. Use what you have learned about wisdom in this study so far as well as the scriptures that talk about wisdom and understanding. Make your writing a story or poem. When completed insert it into your binder for this chapter.

Activity 6 – Foolishness is the opposite of wisdom. If you like art assign colors to each of these words and create an abstract piece of art showing the differences. When completed insert it into your binder for this chapter.

Activity 7 – Here are some real-life situations. Imagine these scenarios and write what you think possible outcomes could be for a wise choice and a foolish choice.

- You have a big project due tomorrow. You have worked on it a bit, but not enough. You really want to finish playing your video game, but it is getting late.

    The Wise Choice _____

    The Foolish Choice _____

- Your friends invite you to a party. You want to go because the popular kids at school will be there and you do not get invited often. You are a bit concerned because the popular kids sometimes drink when their parents are not looking.

    The Wise Choice _____

    The Foolish Choice _____

- You are taking a test and get stuck on a few of the questions. You studied hard for days and now you are blanking. You know you know the right answers, but nothing is coming to mind. The smart kid in class is sitting next to you and you can easily see what is on his paper.

    The Wise Choice _____

    The Foolish Choice _____

Activity 8 – Pick one verse for wisdom and one verse for foolishness. Combine them to make a song or a rap. Include what God is trying to teach in the verses.

Chapter Eleven

Forgiveness vs. Anger

MONTHLY PLANNING PAGE

MONTH _____ CHARACTER TRAIT _____ PITFALL _____

HOMEWORK SECTION COMPLETED
(insert on each line below the homework sections you will complete for this trait)

WEEK 1
_____ MENTOR _____
_____ ☐ ☐ ☐ ☐
_____ DATES WE MEET _____
_____

WEEK 2
_____ MEMORY VERSE _____
_____ ☐ ☐ ☐ ☐
_____ HISTORICAL FIGURE _____
_____ BIOGRAPHY/AUTOBIOGRAPGY TITLE (if applicable) _____

WEEK 3
_____ SEXUAL PURITY STUDY GUIDE TITLE (if applicable) _____
_____ ☐ ☐ ☐ ☐
_____ SERVICE PROJECTS (if applicable) _____
_____ _____

WEEK 4
_____ DATES PROJECTS COMPLETED _____
_____ ☐ ☐ ☐ ☐
_____ _____
_____ NOTES, PAPERS, RESEARCH INSERTED IN BINDER:

YES   NO

Godly Trait – Forgiveness

Martin Luther King, Jr. once said, "Forgiveness does not mean ignoring what has been done or putting a false label on an evil act. It means, rather, that the evil act no longer remains as a barrier to the relationship. Forgiveness is a catalyst creating the atmosphere necessary for a fresh start and a new beginning." (17)

Forgiving someone who has wronged us is incredibly difficult. Somewhere inside of us we desire justice; we want people to pay for their mistakes and get what they deserve. Often, we want them to hurt the way they hurt us. It is a natural tendency to want to remind them of what they have done and bring it up again the next time we are hurt. But as children of God, we are called to a higher standard. Forgiveness is required for us to not only live at peace with those around us but with God himself. We will look at the effect of harboring bitterness and choosing anger, later in this study, but for now let's look at what God says about forgiveness and the benefits of making this choice.

Scripture Study

Psalm 79:9
Help us, God our Savior, for the glory of your name; deliver us and forgive our sins for your name's sake.

Matthew 6:12, 14
And forgive us our debts, as we also have forgiven our debtors. For if you forgive other people when they sin against you, your heavenly Father will also forgive you.

Luke 17:4
Even if they sin against you seven times in a day and seven times come back to you saying 'I repent,' you must forgive them."

Colossians 3:13
Bear with each other and forgive one another if any of you has a grievance against someone. Forgive as the Lord forgave you.

 # Biblical Figure Study

There are so many characters in the Bible and parables that speak to forgiveness, too many to mention. Here are a few that stand out.

<u>Joseph</u> – Read Genesis 50

You are probably familiar with the story; his brothers grew to hate him because of the visions he had of them bowing down to him. Rather than kill him, which was their first choice, they decided to sell him to slave traders. Joseph ends up in Egypt in the house of Potiphar. Over the course of many years he is falsely accused, put in jail, forgotten, betrayed. All these horrible things happened because his brothers sold him into slavery. Joseph had many reasons to be bitter and angry. Yet, when presented with an opportunity to forgive his brothers he does it!! Not only does he forgive but he acknowledges that what was meant for evil God used for good. He sees the good that has come from the bad.

<u>The Prodigal Son</u> – Read Luke 15:11-32

In this parable the younger son gives his father many reasons to be angry. The father chooses forgiveness instead, restoring the son back to the family.

Pitfall – Sinful Anger/Bitterness

Godly anger is righteous anger at the injustice in the world, such as evil actions against innocent people, child abuse, violence, etc. But the pitfall we are learning about here is sinful anger. When a person chooses to harbor bitterness in their heart due to hurts or unresolved conflict, misunderstandings, and pain, bitterness sets in. When we let our anger fester rather than addressing the valid emotion we feel, we harden our heart rather than forgive.

　In his book *A Gentle Answer*, author Scott Sauls says, "Like a poisonous berry, vindictiveness tastes sweet and swallows smoothly at first. But once it gets into you, it starts working less like fruit and more like cyanide. To survive it, we must expunge it from our system." [18]

Scripture Study

Matthew 6:15
But if you do not forgive others their sins, your Father will not forgive your sins.

Ephesians 4:31
Get rid of all bitterness, rage and anger, brawling and slander, along with every form of malice.

Hebrews 12:15
See to it that no one falls short of the grace of God and that no bitter root grows up to cause trouble and defile many.

Biblical Figure Study

Cain – Read Genesis 4:2-8
"Later she gave birth to his brother Abel. Now Abel kept flocks, and Cain worked the soil. In the course of time Cain brought some of the fruits of the soil as an offering to the LORD. And Abel also brought an offering – fat portions from some of the firstborn of his flock. The LORD looked with favor on Abel and his offering, but on Cain and his offering he did not look with favor. So Cain was very angry, and his face was downcast. Then the LORD said to Cain, "Why are you angry? Why is your face downcast? If you do what is right, will you not be accepted? But if you do not do what is right, sin is crouching at your door; it desires to have you, but you must rule over it." Now Cain said to his brother Abel, "Let's go out to the field." While they were in the field, Cain attacked his brother Abel and killed him.

Cain and Abel, sons of Adam and Eve, both presented the Lord with their offerings. The difference between the two was that Cain did not give the best of his fruits and Abel gave the best of his flocks, the firstborn. God looked with favor on Abel but rebuked Cain. It was not because God preferred livestock over plant offerings. It was because Cain did not offer the best of his crops, merely some of them. Cain was angry at Able for receiving God's favor and let his anger toward his brother fester. He did the unthinkable

Esau – Read Genesis 27:1-41

Jacob and Esau, like Cain and Abel, were brothers. Jacob, younger only by a bit, wanted the birthright and blessing that was reserved for the oldest son. In his selfishness and greed, he agreed to a scheme designed by his mom, to trick old, blind dad Isaac, into giving Jacob the blessing. When it was official, and Esau was deceived out of what was rightfully his, he became enraged. Jacob fled for his life.

Forgiveness vs. Anger Homework

1. The story of Joseph from the biblical figure study is an amazing story of the power of forgiveness. If anyone had the right to carry a grudge and be angry it was Joseph. Hated by his brothers, thrown into a pit to die, then sold into slavery, falsely accused of rape, put in prison, forgotten—that is a tough set of circumstances to overcome. All these things happened because of the evil choice made by angry and bitter brothers. Has anything bad happened to you because of someone else's choice, resulting in circumstances out of your control? If so, explain below. What was your response to this situation?

2. In Luke 15:11-32, the story of the prodigal son, why do you think it was possible for the father to forgive his son? Do you think it was easy? Has there been something significant you have done that required the forgiveness of your parents or a close friend? Write out what you are comfortable sharing. What was the result of their forgiveness for you?

3. The pitfall biblical figure studies are quite extreme. In both cases, Cain and Esau had murderous intent in their heart because they let their anger turn into bitterness. Most of the time, (and hopefully it is all the time), our anger does not reach that extreme. However, we can harbor bitterness and choose to hold on to an unforgiving spirit, to pay someone back for the wrong they have done to us. Have you ever done this? Explain why and how it made you feel to hold onto your anger.

4. If you have been raised in a Christian home and have grown up attending church, you may have heard more than once that God forgives our sins when we confess them to him. Also, he does not hold our sin against us. These are true statements. Yet, look at Matthew 6:15 again. It appears to contradict these truths. Do a little bit of research, either a Google search or using a Bible commentary (book form if you have access to one, or an online commentary for this verse. Search "Bible commentary Matthew 6:15") and see if you can identify the true meaning behind this verse. Write out your discoveries below.

5. Why do you think Joseph was able to get to a place of forgiveness? What was the result of his choice to forgive? Can you speculate what would have happened if he chose to hold on to his anger?

6. Listen to the song "Forgiveness"[19] by Christian music artist Matthew West on YouTube. Does this song stir up any emotion for you? Write your thoughts here. The YouTube link for your reference is listed as #19 on the Citation page in the back of the book.

7. Choose a verse from the Scripture study on forgiveness and commit it to memory. Reference it here and record it on your monthly planning page.

Becoming a Woman of Forgiveness

Hey gals, the following questions are just for you. Take the time to work through them being as honest as you can.

1. Middle school and high school are tough for girls. There is peer pressure all around (even if you are in a homeschool situation you will find the pressure of your peers in your co-op, church youth group, neighborhood, etc.). Social media is a huge influence, including TV, movies, magazines, and internet content. It is easy to hurt others in comparing ourselves to one another, and even easier to be hurt by what others say about us. Do you find that forgiveness, even among family members, is easy or hard for you? Do you struggle to release the obligation of your friends or siblings to pay for the hurtful things they have done?

2. As you grow into adulthood, and hopefully continue to pursue godliness, you will experience hurt in many ways. Your husband will hurt your feelings. Your children will disrespect you. Your co-workers will criticize you. Your parents, yes, your parents, will interfere (out of love of course 😊). Your friends will disappoint. Learning to forgive is crucial if you do not want to carry around the burden of anger. How would staying angry affect these relationships?

Sometimes a hurt is so deep that it may take a while to forgive (abuse, slandering your reputation, betrayal). The Bible does not teach us to ignore the hurts and pretend all is well.

It is okay to take some time to deal with the hurt, process it, even get counseling if that is required. Being able to come back to the person who hurt you with a whole heart allows for complete forgiveness. But refusing to forgive so that you can keep dwelling on the hurt does a few things. It makes you miserable. The other person has likely moved on, but you are the one who is angry. It allows bitterness to set in which can impede your relationship with that person and with the Lord. It also allows you to continue to blame the offender. None of these things honor the Lord. Pray the Lord gives you a soft heart that easily forgives and one humble enough to ask for forgiveness.

Becoming a Man of Forgiveness

Hey guys, the following questions are just for you. Take the time to work through them being as honest as you can.

1. Most people like to be right. When you are hurt or offended by something, you likely feel that this wrong needs to be made right. The offender needs to see the error of their ways and make amends. Justice needs to be served. This is a natural response. However, it is not always our place to correct the wrongs done to us. Sometimes forgiveness needs to be extended even if our offender does not ask for it. What does forgiving someone without their repentance do for you? Think of Jesus on the cross in Luke 23:33-34. Does his example shape your thinking?

2. As you grow into adulthood, and hopefully continue to pursue godliness, how will the habit of forgiveness you establish now be important as you think through your grown-up relationships? Can you think of ways you would need to extend forgiveness to a wife, children, co-workers, ministry partners, neighbors, or friends?

Sometimes a hurt is so deep that it may take a while to forgive (abuse, slandering your reputation, betrayal). The Bible does not teach us to ignore the hurts and pretend all is well. It is ok to take some time to deal with the hurt, process it, even get counseling if that is required. Being able to come back to the person who hurt you with a whole heart allows for complete forgiveness. But refusing to forgive so that you can keep dwelling on the hurt does a few things. It makes you miserable. The other person has likely moved on, but you are the one who is angry. It allows bitterness to set in which can impede your relationship with that person and with the Lord. It also allows you to continue to blame the offender. None of these things honor the Lord. Pray the Lord gives you a soft heart that easily forgives and one humble enough to ask for forgiveness.

Historical Figure

Chose a person (past or present) whom you feel exhibits qualities of forgiveness. You may choose from the list provided in the resource guide in Part Four of this book or select one of your own. Do some research on the person (internet search, library books) and answer the following questions:

1. Why did you choose this individual?

2. What aspect of forgiveness do they exhibit?

3. Explain how they lived this out in their daily life.

4. Do they have moments of anger? Explain.

Biography/Autobiography

If you like to read, select a biography or autobiography on this individual to read throughout this month. Your parent may ask you to provide a book report or synopsis (personal choice for format) on what you read, paying special attention to their commitment to live a life of forgiveness.

 ## Media Option

Is there a movie or documentary on the historical person you chose? If so, take some time to watch it and write down several things you can identify about how they lived out forgiveness.

 ## Mentoring

Choose a mentor who exhibits qualities of forgiveness that you or your parents admire. Get together (how often is up to you, but often one meeting is sufficient as there are many other mentors involved in this process) and listen as they share their life experiences with you. Your parent(s) will help guide the content of your discussions along with your mentor's ideas. If your mentor provides charts, lists, or diagrams as visuals, insert them into your binder for this chapter, along with any notes you may take. Possible discussion questions may include:

- Hurts in my life I have had to forgive…
- Why it is hard to forgive sometimes…
- The blessings that have resulted in my choosing forgiveness…
- Times I have asked for forgiveness and they said no…

Journal Page

1. What, if anything, did the Lord imprint on your heart during your study of forgiveness?

2. Are there areas of your life you need to confess and receive forgiveness? Take some time to write those things down and confess your sin to the Lord. Let his forgiveness wash over you!

3. Is there someone you need to forgive, but you have been hanging on to your anger? Pray about that person then call them or meet them in person and extend forgiveness. Write out the result of this interaction.

4. Spend some time in prayer talking to God about what you have learned, including the lessons you learned from your mentor. Ask the Lord to give you the courage to forgive even when it is hard, knowing how much he has already forgiven you.

5. Review your memory verse.

Alternative Learning Pages
Do all or some of the following 8 activities

Activity 1 – Read, or have someone read for you, the following portions about the life of Joseph from the Biblical figure study. Genesis 37:12-36, Genesis 39 and 40. These are long chapters so break this up over a couple days if you need to. Make a list below of all the things that happened to Joseph because of his brothers' original choice.

1 _____

2 _____

3 _____

4 _____

5 _____

6 _____

Activity 2 – Read, or have someone read for you, Genesis 45:1-14. This is Joseph's response to his brothers when they discovered who he was. How do you think he was able to achieve such a soft heart after all his suffering? Write your answer below or have a parent write for you.

_____

_____

_____

Activity 3 – Listen to the following song, "Forgiveness" [19] by Christian music artist, Matthew West on YouTube with your parent's permission. Does anything come to mind as it relates to your need to forgive others? Is there something you might need to make right with someone else that needs forgiving?

_____

_____

_____

Activity 4 – Do the following crossword puzzle

ACROSS
3. What you hold against someone
6. Murdered his brother
7. That thing done to us that is hurtful
8. How God viewed Abel's offering
10. Releasing a person from the penalty of their actions
13. Holding on to your anger and letting it fester
15. Not giving us what our sins deserve

DOWN
1. Turning away from sin
2. What Jacob did to Esau
4. The best of a crop or herd
5. Spending money recklessly or extravagantly
9. Stole his brother's blessing
11. What the brothers did to Joseph
12. Imprisoned for something he did not do
14. Support structure for a plant embedded deep underground

Activity 5 – Think back over this last week. Did you have any interactions with your family where you were disobedient, disrespectful, rude, or insensitive? Jot down a few of those situations here. As you go throughout the week try to apologize and ask for forgiveness.

_____

_____

_____

_____

Activity 6 – Look at the story of Jacob and Esau in Genesis 27:1-41. Imagine a different outcome for Jacob if Esau had continued to hate his brother and refused to forgive. If you like to draw, illustrate what that interaction might have looked like. If you prefer creative writing, write, or have someone write for you, how this story would have ended differently. When completed, insert your drawing or writing into your binder for this chapter.

Activity 7 – If you like making art, using any medium you choose (paint, draw, color, cut/paste, build with blocks, clay), create a piece that depicts the concept of forgiveness. You can portray the emotions around anger and forgiveness, it can be a picture of a certain situation, you can use words only to form a design. Get creative. When complete, if you can insert into your binder, do so. If it is not insertable, take a picture of your completed masterpiece, print it, and insert into your binder for this chapter. Be sure to explain your art to your family.

Activity 8 – Choose one of the verses on Forgiveness from the scripture study above. Explain to your parent(s) what you believe it means and why you chose that verse. Write it out on a notecard and stick it to your mirror so you can see it and review it every day.

PART THREE

CEREMONY AND CELEBRATIONS

Celebrating your child completing this curriculum is important. Whether they took a school year to complete or an abbreviated four months, their accomplishment needs to be celebrated. This is an intense, thorough study and has required time and effort, not just for your child but for you as the parent(s). If you feel your child is ready to be launched into biblical man/womanhood, let us talk about different ways you can have a ceremony to commemorate this huge milestone.

Celebrations can be as simple or elaborate as you choose. The important thing here is celebrating the milestone of completing the rigorous program and commemorating their entrance into godly adulthood. How you do that will be unique to your family. Ceremonies or celebrations of any kind are completely optional, however, highly recommended.

Celebration Options

The type of ceremony you have for your child will depend on:
- your family situation
- the personality of your child (extrovert or introvert)
- special needs considerations
- time constraints

Here are some options for most scenarios:

1. Informal:

Informal celebrations are good for the shy child that prefers to remain behind the scenes, families who do not have a lot of free time, parents who do not like event planning, or kids with special needs that might require greater accommodations.

- Make a special meal together or go out to a favorite restaurant. Take some time during the meal to talk about the child's accomplishment and some of their highlights. Create a certificate of completion and present it to your child and acknowledge their journey to biblical man or womanhood.
- Videoconference with long distance relatives and allow them to share their love and words of blessing for a job well done. Have your child share a couple of highlights or things they learned and present a certificate of program completion and their journey to godly adulthood.
- Encourage friends, family members and mentors to send your child a special card or a small gift to acknowledge their accomplishment. You can post these in their room so they can see them every day. Purchase a plaque or engrave their name on a new Bible in recognition of their journey to godly man or womanhood.
- Hold an intimate gathering in your home where the child, if they are comfortable, can share what they have been learning or you as the parent can give a summary. This evening could incorporate videos, special prayers, and fun activities that your child

likes. If your child is very shy, record them answering questions about what they learned and play the video during the gathering. Acknowledge their journey to godly adulthood and present them with certificate or other memorabilia.

- **For sons specifically**: A weekend camping getaway with the guys (dad, brothers, male mentors, good buddies). Good conversations around the fire, hiking, fishing, etc., could be special ways of connecting and discussing deeper things of the Lord. Intentional "coming of age" themes can make it memorable.
    - If any mentors are local invite them take a night around the fire and share highlights of their conversations with your son with the group. Also have them share personal stories of their own journey to godly manhood, how God shaped them, disciplined them, made them leaders.
    - Give your son an opportunity, during a walk or other activity, to share the things he learned and verses memorized.
    - Have dad or a pastor, if attending, have the group lay hands on your son and pray prayers of blessing, commitment, consecration, encouragement over him.
    - Have dad or a pastor, if attending, present your son with a new Bible or a "Young Man's Devotional" to commemorate the milestone of godly manhood.

- **For daughters specifically**: A weekend tea party/spa theme with the ladies (mom, sisters, female mentors, girlfriends). Good conversations as you prepare meals, get your nails done, take walks, sit by the pool, could be special ways of connecting and discussing deeper things of the Lord. Intentional "coming of age" themes can make it memorable.
    - If any mentors are local and in attendance, have them each take an opportunity around a meal or a walk and share highlights of their conversations with your daughter with the group. Also encourage women to share their personal stories of godly womanhood and how they have journeyed with the Lord.
    - Give your daughter an opportunity to share things she learned, highlights of the program, and verses she memorized.
    - Have mom or a female friend or youth leader, if attending, have the group lay hands on your daughter and pray prayers of blessing, commitment, consecration, and encouragement over her.
    - Have mom or a female friend, if attending, present your daughter with a new Bible or a "Young Woman's Devotional" to commemorate the milestone of godly womanhood.

NOTE: If you chose any of the first three informal celebrations, they require little to no planning and can be done any time after completing the program. The last three options, the intimate gathering and weekend getaways for guys or girls, are informal in nature but would require some planning to coordinate with guests and chose a location.

2. Formal:

Formal celebrations usually take on the feel of a ceremony. They are great for the more outgoing child who does not mind being in front of people, the parent who has more time to plan a larger gathering, or families who enjoy event planning and are detail oriented.

   A. Types of Formal Ceremonies
- Party with a Program:
  Make it a semi-formal event, inviting family, friends, mentors, and your child's friends. Create a program to include time for you and your child to do a Q & A about what they learned in each trait they studied, and the Bible verses memorized. Include prayers of blessing from pastors or youth leaders as well as from parents and grandparents if they can attend. You could serve food, either a sit- down meal, appetizers, or desserts. Create places for attendees to write notes of encouragement or a blessing to your child. Decorations and music are nice touches.

- Church Event:
  If you are doing this program with a group of friends from church, ask your church leadership if you can use the gym or fellowship hall to host a group ceremony. If you have included your pastors in the process, they may want to advertise it to the congregation and encourage a larger gathering to support you. The program and ceremony components could be like the one listed above.

- Graduation Ceremony/Party:
  This could be conducted much like an open house graduation party. Guests could come and go during a specified time frame. Tables could be set up with pictures of your child's service opportunities, meetings with mentors, homework samples, the biographies or other book(s) read, a poster of all the character traits listed, and Bible verses learned. The biblical and historical characters studied could also be displayed. Make a video of you "interviewing" your child with a Q & A of the highlights and lowlights of their journey and play it on a loop. Set out goodies for guests to enjoy and hang balloons or other festive décor. Create places for guests to write encouraging notes or blessings for your child to read after the event is over.

If you choose a formal ceremony it may help to decide on a date before starting the curriculum. When you have selected your date, work your way backwards to determine your program start time. You may want a few weeks to a month, after completing the last character trait, to review all your child has learned before having your celebration.

Formal events such as these would require invitations and advanced planning. Following are ideas for how to plan for a formal event.

B. Formal Ceremony Components and Instructions

If you go the formal route and need help putting together the components for a big event, here is a list of things to consider as you prepare. These are suggestions to get you thinking of what your ceremony could include:

- Decide on the date - When can out-of-town guests attend, is there a school break (spring break, summer break) that makes it easier for friends to come?
- Venue – Choose a location big enough for guests and whatever type of program you have. Church basements, community clubhouses, your backyard, or school auditoriums are good choices.
  - ❖ Is there a rental fee involved?
  - ❖ Is it large enough for guests to mingle, sit, or stand at tables?
  - ❖ What is provided and what do you need to provide? Tables, chairs, tablecloths, sound equipment? Can you borrow these or is renting required?
  - ❖ Is there access to a kitchen to prepare food if needed?
- Guest list – How many attendees you can have may be limited by the size of your venue. Consider immediate family, grandparents, mentors, close friends, friends of your child (which may or may not include their parents/families), pastors, and youth leaders.
- Create an invitation - Shutterfly, Costco Photo, and other online companies have great, easy to use sites for creating invitations. You can always make your own and print up copies. If you do not want a formal invitation, an email is sufficient or an Evite option for digital invites.
  - ❖ Include the date, time, location, and what they should wear (if you want it to be more formal). Mail/email them with plenty of time for folks to plan. A month is a suitable time frame.
- Food or no food – Will you want appetizers and desserts or a full meal? Will you serve finger foods or items that need cutlery? Based on food selections, determine what types of plastic utensils, beverage containers, etc. you will need. The kind of food will also dictate if you need tables at which to sit, or if guests will stand at bistro tables, etc.
  - ❖ If you have a large group attending, consider hiring a server or ask a friend to manage the food distribution. They will make sure beverage containers are full, food is plated and refreshed, add ice to drinks, etc. If you serve food during a social time, you will want to be free to visit with people and not be stuck in the kitchen.
- Traffic flow - Arrange your space to accommodate traffic flow. If you have a big enough space, you can have food tables on one side and seating areas on the other. You could also have tall bistro tables around the perimeter and the seating areas for the program (if you have one) in the middle of the room.

- Printed program - Would you like guests to have a printed "order of program" to follow along during the event? If so, decide if you will make your own or have them printed for you. Office supply stores can print programs.
- Decorations or no decorations – Nice décor throughout the venue creates a festive atmosphere. Ideas include balloons, streamers, flowers, sports memorabilia, string lights, family Bible, artificial or live plants (some venues may have this already for you to borrow).
- Live music or music of any kind – Background music (live or recorded) could be played as people arrive, mingle, and eat. If your child is musical and willing, it is an excellent idea to have them sing or play a song that has some meaning based on the themes of their study. This could be done during the program portion of the event.
- Timing - When will you have the program portion of the event and what do you want to include? Program ideas to consider are:
  - ❖ Interview style Q&A with your child about each trait they studied and what they learned
  - ❖ Introduce mentors
  - ❖ Highlights of their times with their mentors
  - ❖ Tributes by parent(s) and/or grandparent(s)
  - ❖ Prayers for your child by pastors, grandparents, parents
  - ❖ Musical selections
  - ❖ Videos of their service opportunities
  - ❖ Devotional by a pastor or youth leader
- Add meaningful touches -
  - ❖ A blessing tree – provide small slips of paper with holes punched in each and pieces of string. Guests can write a blessing to your child and tie it to the tree branches (use an actual tree cutting).
  - ❖ A blessing jar – same idea as above but place the written blessings in a jar.
  - ❖ Poster for guests to sign and give a wish or blessing for your child
  - ❖ Family Bible displayed
  - ❖ Framed picture of your child
  - ❖ Calligraphy signs or posters with the character traits listed
  - ❖ Photos of your child with their mentors or serving
  - ❖ Photo spot for guests to take pictures with your child or just of themselves
- "After-party" activity – You may want to consider an after-party activity. For the boys, a pick-up game of basketball or soccer, if there is such a space, with the dads and buddies. For the girls, a dance party, or fun craft idea. A group movie could be fun.

C. Celebration Planning

   Use the following pages to help you organize your thoughts and plans for a formal ceremony.

CELEBRATION PLANNING PAGES

Date of celebration/ceremony _____ Type of Celebration _____

Venue _____ Rental fee _____

What is provided _____

What I need to provide _____

Informal event info:
Activities:

Certificate, plaque, other form of program completion award _____

Formal event info:
Floor Plan (a general sketch of table placement, décor placement, chairs for program, front/back of the room)

Food

Decorations

_____   _____
_____   _____
_____   _____

Meaningful touches

_____   _____
_____   _____
_____   _____

Guest List

_____ _____ _____
_____ _____ _____
_____ _____ _____
_____ _____ _____
_____ _____ _____
_____ _____ _____
_____ _____ _____

Invitation ideas/ordering info

_____
_____
_____

Program elements (order of program)   and participant – include times

_____   _____
_____   _____
_____   _____
_____   _____

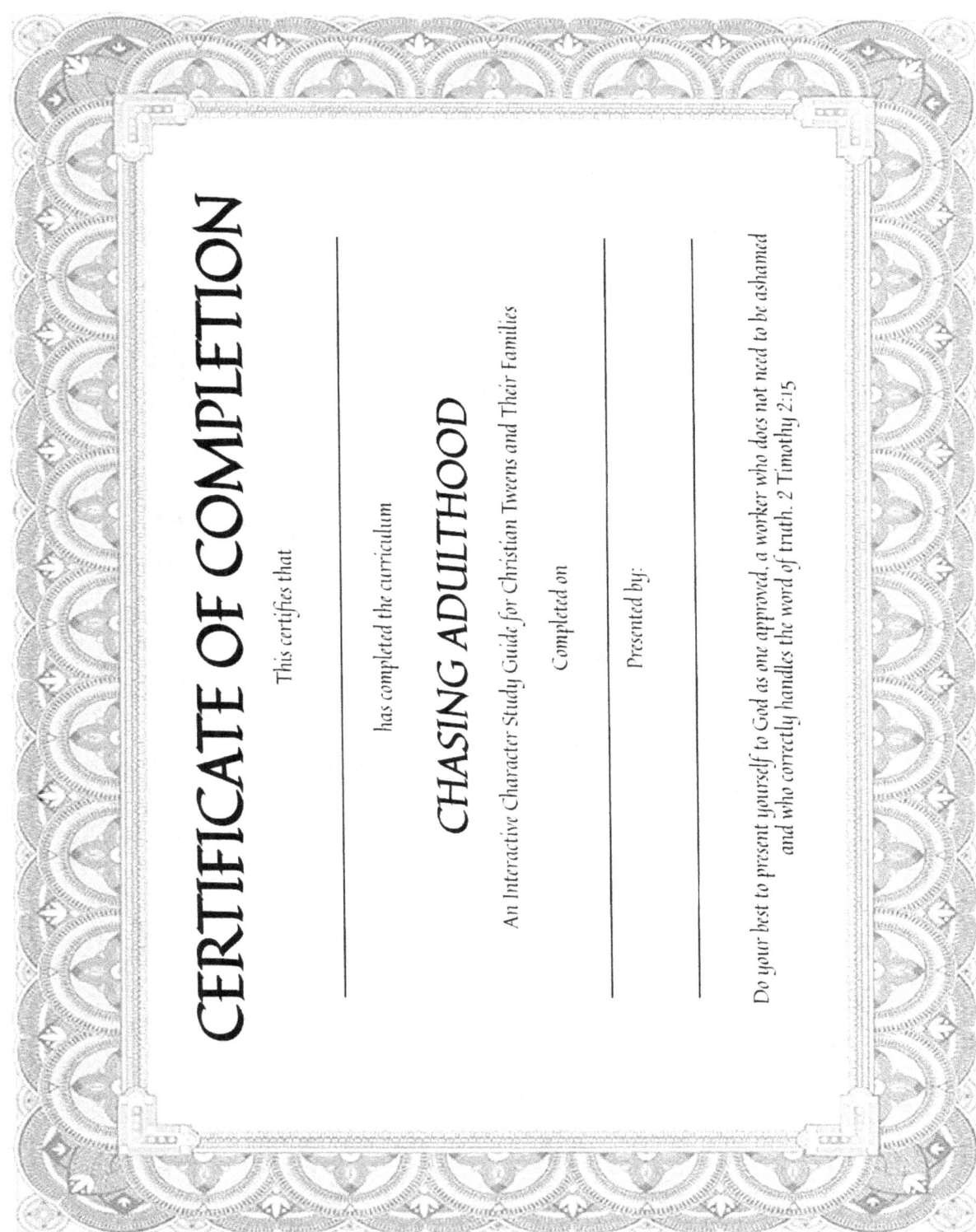

PART FOUR

1. Lists

A. Biblical Figures and Corresponding Godly Traits or Pitfalls

Female Bible Figures with Godly Traits		Female Bible Figures with Pitfall Traits		Male Bible Figures with Godly Traits		Male Bible Figures with Pitfall Traits	
Character	Trait	Character	Trait	Character	Trait	Character	Trait
Mary (Mother of Jesus)	Obedience Faith	Delilah	Deception Dishonesty	David	Obedience Courage Leadership	David	Infidelity Lust
Elizabeth (Mother of John the Baptist)	Faithfulness	Rebecca	Deception Doubted God Jealousy	Abraham	Obedience Faith	Abraham	Doubting God Dishonesty
Ruth	Obedience Loyalty Faith	Potiphar's Wife	Infidelity Deception	Moses	Leadership Obedience	Moses	Disobedience
Deborah	Leadership Courage	Lot's Wife	Doubted God Disobedience	Joshua	Obedience Faithfulness Leadership	Pharisees	Pride Hypocrisy
Esther	Obedience, Purity Integrity, Courage	Jezebel	Prostitution Idol Worship	Daniel	Faith, Purity Discipline, Courage	Nebuchadnezzar	Pride
Lydia	Hospitality	Eve	Doubted God Deception	Joseph	Courage Faithfulness, Purity Self-control, Integrity Forgiveness	King Saul	Disobedience
Martha	Service Hospitality	Bathsheba	Infidelity	Gideon	Courage Faith	Jonah	Disobedience Doubting God
Sarah	Patience	Sarah	Doubted God Jealousy	Paul	Obedience Courage	Cain	Anger
Tabitha	Service			Good Samaritan	Compassion	Esau	Anger
Persistent Widow	Determination Faith			Noah	Determination Faith	Matthew (Tax Collector)	Dishonesty
Mary Magdalene	Loyalty			Job	Patience Faith	Pharaoh	Pride
Hannah	Self-Control Faith, Patience			Stephen	Faithfulness Courage	Judas	Cowardice
Shulamite Woman	Faith Hospitality			Nehemiah	Determination Self-Control		
Rahab	Courage	Rahab	Prostitution	Peter	Faithfulness	Peter	Cowardice

B. Godly Traits and Pitfalls with Corresponding Biblical Figures

Godly Traits

Obedience	Self-Control	Patience	Faithfulness	Leadership	Courage	Faith	Discipline
Mary (Mother of Jesus) Esther David Abraham Joshua Paul Ruth Moses	Hannah Joseph Nehemiah	Job Sarah Hannah	Joshua Joseph Peter Stephen Elizabeth (Mother of John the Baptist)	Joshua David Deborah Moses	Deborah Daniel Esther Rahab David Joseph Gideon Stephen Paul	Ruth Shulamite Woman Hannah Gideon Daniel Abraham Job Noah Persistent Widow Mary (Mother of Jesus)	Daniel
Determination	**Integrity**	**Purity**	**Hospitality**	**Service**	**Compassion**	**Forgiveness**	**Loyalty**
Nehemiah Noah	Joseph Esther	Joseph Esther	Lydia Martha Shulamite Woman	Tabitha Martha	Good Samaritan	Joseph	Ruth Mary Magdalene

Pitfall Traits

Disobedience	Pride	Anger	Lust, Infidelity, Prostitution	Deception, Dishonesty
Lot's Wife Moses Jonah King Saul	Nebuchadnezzar Pharisees Pharoah	Cain Esau	Potiphar's Wife Bathsheba Jezebel Rahab David	Delilah Potiphar's Wife Eve Rebecca Abraham Matthew (the Tax collector)
Jealousy	**Hypocrisy**	**Idol Worship**	**Cowardice**	**Doubting God**
Sarah Rebecca	Pharisees	Jezebel	Peter Judas	Rebecca Lot's Wife Sarah Eve Abraham Jonah

C. Historical Figures

George Washington – President of the US
Abraham Lincoln – President of the US
Ronald Reagan – President of the US
Barak Obama – President of the US
Condolezza Rice – Female US Secretary of State
Hilary Clinton – Female US Secretary of State
Kamela Harris –Female US Vice President
Winston Churchill – Prime Minister of Britain
Queen Elizabeth II – Queen of England
Nelson Mandela – Prime Minister of South Africa
Martin Luther King – Civil rights activist
Mahatma Ghandi – Indian lawyer, civil rights activist, political ethicist
Mother Theresa – Humanitarian
Martin Luther – Theology Professor
Albert Einstein – Theoretical physicist
Harriet Tubman – American abolitionist
Marie Curie – Famous physicist/chemist
Princess Diana – British Royalty, humanitarian
Corrie Ten Boom – Christian, concentration camp survivor
Malala Yousafzai – Indian girl, female rights activist
Ding Limei – Chinese Missionary
Erik Liddell – Athlete, missionary
Amy Carmichael – Missionary
George Mueller – Missionary
Hudson Taylor - Missionary
Jim Elliot – Pilot, Missionary, martyr
C.S. Lewis – Christian author
Nabeel Qureshi – Muslim convert, speaker, author
Jeremy Affeldt – Athlete
Stephen Curry – Athlete
Gailin Emore – Athlete
Chris Tomlin – Musician, worship artist
Jeremy Camp – Musician, worship artist
Lauren Daigle – Musician, worship artist
Mark Lawrence – Painter
Pablo Picaso – Painter
Vincent van Gogh – Painter
Maya Angelou – Poet
Lewis Carroll - Poet
Fred Rogers – American TV personality
Scott Hamilton – Ice Skater
Tara Lipinski – Ice Skater
Tatyana McFadden – Athlete, eleven-time Paralympic medalist

Billy Graham – Christian Evangelist
Horatio Spafford – American Lawyer, hymn writer
Steve Jobs – Founder of Apple
Bill Gates – Founder of Microsoft
Jeff Bezos – Founder of Amazon
Robert Pierce – American Baptist Minister, founder of World Vision International
Henry Ford – founder of Ford Motor Company
Nathan Sawaya – LEGO master builder
Truett Cathy – Christian businessman, founder of Chick-Fil-A
John D. Rockefeller – Christian businessman
David Green – Christian businessman, founder of Hobby Lobby

These character lists are not exhaustive. The historical people referenced were selected because they have accomplished something noteworthy or stand out in some way in their profession. It is not suggested, in any way, that they have godly character, possess a positive reputation, or are Christians. Please use your best judgement in studying the people referenced above.

2. ADDITIONAL RESOURCES

A. Character Trait Resources:

The following are not exhaustive lists but are a few online resources you can use in adding to your character study. These resources, either online or in book form, are <u>not</u> endorsements or recommendations. Please use your own judgement when looking for additional resources for your study.

Online Resources:

- 49 Godly Character Qualities by Grace Online Library - bit.ly/38cG3mJ
  This website gives forty-nine character traits, their opposite trait, a definition, and a scripture reference.

- Discipleship Tools – bit.ly/3PFCVRp
  This website provides excellent information on curriculum for discipleship, studies, and training. Click around at the links at the top of the page to explore all the resources. The link above is an article on what discipleship looks like, what character is, and provides Biblical examples.

- 9 Essential Qualities of a Godly Leader by Brent Rinehart – bit.ly/3lBOMSB
  Though this article speaks specifically about godly leadership a lot of these qualities are traits we as Christian parents would want to see in our kids.

- 5 Character Traits of a Godly Man – bit.ly/3sTaNjU; bit.ly/3yUlsxu
  Two different articles that discuss various character traits in godly men. Both include Scripture references and character support.

- 5 Character Traits of a Godly Woman – bit.ly/3sUBrZL
  An article that lists 5 traits of godly women and includes Scripture references.

Books:

- *The Book of Virtues* by William J. Bennett. William Bennett was the Secretary of Education under President Ronald Reagan. In his conversations with teachers, they expressed to him their frustrations in communicating moral principles to their students. He wrote this book as a guide. Though not heavily faith-based, "faith" is one of the virtues discussed in the book. He uses examples of good and bad character from fairytales, literature, history, the Bible, and mythology.
- *Disciplines of a Godly Young Man* by R. Kent Hughes, Carey Hughes, Jonathan Carswell
  A bold call to young men to live out the command of God to live disciplined lives.
- *Man in Demand* by Emily Hunter. Man in Demand covers a wide range of topics from physical grooming to spiritual character.
- *Young Lady's Guide: The Harmonious Development of Christian Character* by Harvey Newcomb. The author addresses topics like spiritual disciplines as well as physical attentiveness and mental cultivation.
- *The Narrow Way: Character Curriculum and Family Bible Devotional* by Pearables
  A family approach to teaching character to children with 140 lessons. Parent/Child interaction.

B. Scripture verses on Godly character:
These online links give verses for various traits you may be looking for. Not an exhaustive list.

- https://www.biblestudytools.com - When you click on this link you can type in any character trait you are looking for and all the verses in the Bible that reference that trait will appear. You can also search that passage for verses in that context or compare the verse to other translations.
- bit.ly/3NuL0pT - This link lists 38 various verses in the Bible that address character. When you click on the tab "verse concepts" to the right of each verse it reveals all the character qualities to which that verse can be applied.
- bit.ly/3yQXOD6 - When you click on this link you can type in any character trait you are looking for and all the verses in the Bible that reference that trait will appear. It uses the ESV version of the Bible.
- https://www.biblegateway.com - In the search bar you can type in names of people in the Bible, Scripture references or key words (courage, faith, etc.) and it will give you the Scripture references that use those words.

C. Biblical Figure resources:
These online links give names of people in the Bible who exhibited certain character traits.

- *Women of the Bible* - bit.ly/3a6yDSz This link directs you to ChristianBook.com where you can order this Bible study. It is a compilation of 52 women in Bible study format.

- *Ten Men of The Bible* - bit.ly/3NuN5lH A Bible study focusing on 10 men of the Bible and their character written by Max Lucado.
- *Ten Women of the Bible* - bit.ly/3PB1rmx Like "Ten Men of the Bible", Max Lucado made a study of 10 women of the Bible.

D. Purity Study Guide resources:
These books have not been personally reviewed. Please be discerning when looking for books of this subject matter, and make sure the content matches your family values and is age appropriate for your child. Not all authors may write from a Biblical perspective. Though the intention was to only include Christ centered materials it is possible not all these resources approach from that vantage point. This is <u>not</u> an endorsement of any book specifically, rather suggestions for research.
**books that are not gender specific

For young ladies:

- *40 Days of Purity* – by Sharie and Clayton King
- *Before You Meet Prince Charming: A Guide to Radiant Purity* - by Sarah Mally (this book has a study guide)
- *And the Bride Wore White: Seven Secrets to Sexual Purity* - by Dannah Gresh
- *Sex, Purity, and the Longings of a Girl's Heart* – by Kristen Clark (Author), Bethany Beal (Author)
- *Passion and Purity*– by Elizabeth Elliot **
- *Talking Back to Purity Culture: Rediscovering Faithful Christian Sexuality* – by Rachel Joy Welcher (Author), Scott Sauls (Foreword) **

For young men:

- *Pornography: Fighting for Purity* – by Deepak Reju
- *40 Days of Purity for Guys* - by Clayton King
- *When Young Men Are Tempted: Sexual Purity for Guys in the Real World* - by William Perkins, Randy Southern
- *Authentic Love - Bible Study for Guys: Christ, Culture, and the Pursuit of Purity* – by D.A. Horton
- *Moral Revolution: The Naked Truth About Sexual Purity* - by Kris Vallotton, Jason Vallotton **
- *Talking with Teens about Sexuality: Critical Conversations about Social Media, Gender*
- *Identity, Same-Sex Attraction, Pornography, Purity, Dating, Etc.* – eBook by Beth Robinson EdD, Latayne C. Scott PhD **
- *Sex Isn't the Problem, Lust Is* – by Joshua Harris
- www.christianbook.com is an excellent online bookstore. Search "purity" in the search bar for more resources. Check out your local Christian Book store for other titles.

E. Purity Ring options:
If you have a Christian bookstore locally, they often carry a selection of rings. Here are some online options.
- bit.ly/3sRl6DX
- bit.ly/3Gg4k8g
- amzn.to/3akhlMz
- bit.ly/3wEtutK
- bit.ly/3wEWrEO

F. LGBTQ+ resources
The following links are for various Christian ministries who have books, podcasts, or other resources that speak to the LGBTQ+ lifestyle and related gender topics. If you are unsure what you believe on this issue or how to address it with your kids, I encourage you to research using some or all of these links. If you attend a Bible believing church your pastor may also have some good resources for you. Pray for discernment on how to address this topic with kindness, grace, and truth.
- http://store.focusonthefamily.com/homosexuality-transgenderism
- https://seanmcdowell.org/podcasts
- www.christianbook.com

3. TEMPLATES

This section includes templates of all the worksheets used in the character trait study section, part two. If you have other character traits you would like to use that are not in the book you can create your own sections. Make copies of the pages you wish to include.
- Chapter Title Page
- Monthly Planning Page
- Godly Trait/Pitfall
- Homework Page
- Historical Figure
- Media Option
- Mentoring
- Journal Page

Alternative Learning Pages are not included with templates. Simply select an activity from other trait studies.

Chapter _____

_____ vs. _____

(insert chapter number and the Godly trait vs. the pitfall trait)

MONTHLY PLANNING PAGE

MONTH _____ CHARACTER TRAIT _____ PITFALL _____

HOMEWORK SECTION   COMPLETED   MENTOR _____
(insert on each line below the homework sections you will complete for this trait)

WEEK 1 ☐☐☐☐   DATES WE MEET _____
_____
_____   MEMORY VERSE _____
_____   HISTORICAL FIGURE _____

WEEK 2 ☐☐☐☐   BIOGRAPHY/AUTOBIOGRAPGY TITLE (if applicable) _____
_____
_____   SEXUAL PURIITY STUDY GUIDE TITLE (if applicable) _____
_____

WEEK 3 ☐☐☐☐   SERVICE PROJECTS (if applicable) _____
_____
_____   _____
_____

WEEK 4 ☐☐☐☐   DATES PROJECTS COMPLETED _____
_____
_____   NOTES, PAPERS, RESEARCH INSERTED IN BINDER:
_____

YES   NO

Godly Trait - _____ (insert character trait)

Description –

Scripture Study – (select several Bible verses that talk about this character trait)

Biblical Figure – (select a Bible figure who exhibited this quality, include the Scripture passages or Bible verses)

Pitfall - _____ (insert the opposite trait)

Description –

Scripture Study – (select several Bible verses that talk about this character trait)

Biblical Figure – (select a Bible figure who exhibited this quality, include the Scripture passages or Bible verses)

_____ vs. _____ **Homework Page Template**

Write 5-6 strong questions as it relates to the biblical figures you chose and the corresponding Scriptures. Girls and Guys questions are optional.

1.

2.

3.

4.

5.

Historical Figure Template

Choose a person from history (past or present) whom you feel exhibits qualities of _____ You may choose from the list provided in the resource guide in Part Four of this book or select one of your own. Do some research on this person (internet search, library books) and answer the following questions:

1. Why did you choose this individual?

_____

_____

2. What aspect of _____ do they exhibit?

_____

3. Explain how they lived this out in their daily life.

_____

_____

_____

4. What obstacles did they have to overcome to maintain this character trait?

_____

_____

_____

Biography/Autobiography

If you like to read, select a biography or autobiography on this individual to read throughout this month. Your parent may ask you to provide a book report or synopsis (personal choice for format) on what you read, paying special attention to their _____ (insert character trait).

Media Option Template

Is there a movie or documentary on the historical figure you chose? If so, take some time to watch it and write down several things you can identify about their life of _____ (insert character trait).

Mentoring Template

Choose a mentor who exhibits qualities of _____ (insert character trait) that you or your parent(s) admire. Get together (how often is up to you, but often one meeting is sufficient as there are many other mentors involved in this process) and listen as they share their life experiences with you. Your parents will help guide the content of your discussions along with your mentor's ideas. If your mentor provides charts, lists, or diagrams as visuals, insert them into your binder for this chapter, along with any notes you may take. Possible discussion questions may include:
- How I live this trait in my life…..
- Times it is hard…
- Times I chose the pitfall of this trait…
- Ways I feel the Lord has blessed me because of this character trait…

Journal Page Template

1. What, if anything, did the Lord imprint on your heart during your study of _____?

2. From the homework page, did you identify any areas in your life that needed work? If so, what action steps might you take to make improvements?

3. What are you willing to give up in order to obtain this character trait?

4. Spend some time in prayer talking to God about what you have learned, and the lessons you learned from your mentor.

5. Review your memory verse.

4. FAQs
(Frequently asked questions)

How can I work this program around my child's traditional school and/or after school activities?

- Find out what kind of time your child has in their schedule. If they typically go from school to activities, do homework then go to bed it will be a lot more challenging to find open space for them to be on board. But it is not impossible.
- Try to identify a few available hours a week where they can work, and where you are available for discussion and input. Weekends may be a good opportunity.
- Take 30 minutes before their bedtime to sit and read together and work through some questions. Often kids are more eager to talk and interact at the end of their busy day.
- During an evening meal is another great time. You could use this hour (or less) as time for the family to interact on the character studies and work through the questions together.
- Encourage their reading of biographies from historical figures who lived their lives exhibiting character traits you want in your kids. If you really cannot find time in your child's week then it is best to set this aside and postpone until their schedule is less hectic.

How can I abbreviate this program to fit into a shorter time frame?

If you are limited in your time or your child cannot commit to a longer period of study, here are some ways to truncate the program yet still make it meaningful.
- Choose three- or four-character traits to cover in a four-month period.
- Encourage your mentors to meet with your child a few times during their specific month as opposed to just once.
- Choose three or four biblical/historical characters for each trait and have them study one a week. Create homework pages to reflect weekly work as opposed to monthly.
- Rather than your child reading a book about a person of their choice (IF book reading is part of what you would like them to do), have them do a bit of research on that person and write a short essay describing their life and how they lived out that specific character quality.
- If a service project is important for your child to do, find something they could participate in weekly or monthly, during the program, as opposed to doing a bigger project at the end.

If we want to celebrate with a "ceremony" but we are not party people, what other ideas do you have for recognizing the hard work of our kids?

- Check out Part Three of this book which is all about the celebration ceremony and different ways you can honor your kids' accomplishments, both in formal and informal ways.

I have a child with special needs or learning difficulties. How can I create an effective program that is meaningful but does not require things like homework, or lots of reading?

- At the end of each character trait chapter there are alternative learning pages for these uniquely challenged kiddos. Chose all or some of those activities to help emphasize the important truths of each trait. Read through the standard learning pages first to see what, if any, your child can do. Then add the alternative activities, as necessary.
- Select fewer character traits to focus on and spend more time on each. The last thing you want to do is overwhelm them. Life is already hard.
- Instead of homework pages/questions, make the content more of a discussion. Read stories together of godly people and ask your own questions as you read.
- As you interact with your child it might work better to be their scribe, recording their answers to questions.
- Watch videos or movies of biblical or historical men/women who did impactful things for Christ. Check out the following websites for kids videos, podcasts, or live streamed stories:
    - https://www.adventuresinodyssey.com/
    - https://nestlearning.com/
    - https://theadventum.com/collections/audio-adventures
- Encourage mentor meetings with people your child feels comfortable with. Keep them light with not a lot of heavy content. Depending on what your child's abilities are it may work best to have these discussions while playing a game, going on walks, shooting hoops, etc. Rather than one session per mentor a few may be necessary to facilitate comfort in speaking about deeper things.
- Your child may only feel comfortable with one mentor. You could have a single person meet with your child, but each time focus on a different trait (for example, a Sunday School teacher or youth leader, favorite uncle or aunt, their best friend's mom or dad – whomever they feel safest with and enjoy being with).
- If you can choose a service project that meets their needs, go with them, and work together (unless they are capable and comfortable doing this on their own or in a group). If an outside project with a group or organization would not work simple tasks around the house, serving siblings, helping mom in the kitchen, working with dad outside are all practical ways to practice serving. Without making it overwhelming, choose something that is somewhat challenging and requires effort and commitment. This will help to instill the idea of service. Again, you will know what your child is capable of.
- Ceremony – reference ceremony section for informal ideas

What types of mentoring sessions can I use with my child?

After you have decided what your character traits are and who the mentors will be you can evaluate which traits you feel will need extra time.
- Consult the mentor and ask what time commitment they have. Can they meet more than once with your child, covering multiple aspects of the character trait? Will you have one mentor per trait? Will a one-time meeting over lunch or a hike be enough? The trait of

sexual purity can be a very extensive learning experience if you choose to have your kids work through a book/study guide with their mentors. Their times together could last for the bulk of the curriculum. Most other mentor sessions can be one or two-time meetings. In-person is best, but it might be necessary to arrange videoconference meetings or just phone calls. Technology makes it all very possible.

There are some character traits not covered in the book that I would like my son/daughter to study. Can I add more traits?

- YES! We always want parents to make this the best possible curriculum for their children. What is included in this book is by no means an exhaustive study. In section three of this resource guide there are several templates for the various sections of the trait study. If you have the time and means to create your own you can take the blank templates and insert your own trait, find your scriptures, create homework questions, and include alternative activities as well. Get a three-ring binder and insert tabs representing each trait you study, you can use this binder for all your chapters and any pages you need to insert.

I am not well-versed in the Bible, I am new in my faith, or I am not a churchgoer. How do I know what is most important for my son or daughter to learn?

- All character traits are important for our children to learn. But not all of them can be covered in a study like this. Go through the chapters and read the descriptions of each trait/pitfall. From there you can prioritize which traits you would like to focus on. For example, your son or daughter may be a naturally kind and compassionate kid who seems to always focus on the needs of others. The chapter on compassion may be one you chose to skip.
- If you do attend a church, we recommend speaking with a pastor or youth leader. Let them know what you are doing and get their input on what characteristics they feel are important for your child to know.
- Do you have a strong Christian friend who is also a parent? Ask them what they would do for their kids if they were to do this program. Maybe ask if they would like to partner with you and do this together. We encourage you to pray a lot and ask the Lord what He wants for your child.
- In the lists section of this resource guide are several online resources you can access that give good information on character traits, supporting Scripture verses and Bible Characters. Read through them and see if you can identity certain qualities you would like to instill in your children. Then select the appropriate chapters in the book to focus on. If those traits are not included in the book, you can create your own pages using the templates in section three of the resource guide.
- Also, feel free to reach out via the member Facebook page at www.facebook.com/groups/ChasingAdulthood We are more than happy to help you talk through your priorities for your children and put together a plan that works for you.

- If you do not attend a church but are interested in joining one, it can be a daunting task to find the one that suits you best. Use the internet to search for Bible believing churches in your area. Not all churches preach the Bible. Look at church websites and read their Statements of Faith to make sure they is aligned with what you believe.

How can I get my church and/or pastors involved in this program?

- If you are looking for the support of your local church, we recommend setting up a meeting with your pastor and/or youth director to share with them what you are doing and ask for their help. They may have additional resources for you and can provide support for you along the way. These leaders may also be good mentors for your child. They may be too busy to be involved heavily but it does not hurt to ask. We imagine, upon hearing of your desires for your child and laying out the process you are undertaking, they would be more than happy to support you with resources, accountability, suggestions, or prayer. After all, what you are doing is a fantastic endeavor.

I do not have a supportive spouse, or I am divorced and not in a good relationship with him/her. How can I do this without their help and support?

- If this is your reality, we are sorry you do not have the support of a spouse. It certainly would make this process easier knowing you are both on the same page and want the same things for your child. However, unless your partner is against this program, you can do this on your own.
- Find support in your friends and family, pastors, or other respected adults. Understand that this is for your children and their personal growth. Hang in there, you are doing a good thing!
- Please visit the member Facebook page for ongoing support and encouragement. We are here to help you navigate the process.
www.facebook.com/groups/ChasingAdulthood

Can I do this program with friends?

- YES! In fact, we highly encourage it. Find one or two other friends who have kids with similar ages and come together to make this a group study. You can all choose the same character traits, or you can do your own. The homework can be unique to each child but service projects, book reading, and scriptures could all be the same. They could study together or on their own. If you have mutual friends, common mentors would be an excellent idea – gathering as a group to hear from someone about a specific trait. Group learning can be more fun and helps with accountability.
- If you need more ideas on how to do a group study, contact us via the member Facebook page and we can work out a good plan for you.
www.facebook.com/groups/ChasingAdulthood

What age is this program best suited for?

- The ideal age is roughly between 12 and 14. As the child enters their teen years, they have reached a certain level of maturity that makes this easier than if the child were ten or even younger. This age is at the crossroads of puberty which is a natural time for conversations of manhood and womanhood. Older high school kids could also benefit depending on their maturity level. You may also have a mature child who is ready to tackle these issues at a younger age. Use your best judgement. You know what is best for them.

Who do I talk to when I have questions?

- Once you purchase this program you will have free access to the Facebook page where you can ask questions, collaborate with other families using the program, get ideas and share successes and concerns. We want to encourage you on your journey and help you every step of the way! www.facebook.com/groups/ChasingAdulthood

PART FIVE
Homework/Alternative Learning Activities Answer Key

Questions with specific answers are given below. Questions with personal open-ended answers are either included with suggested responses (meaning these may or may not be the answers your child provides) or not included at all.

Chapter 1 - Servanthood

Q1. Answers may include: She was a follower of Jesus, she was always helping the poor, she was doing good to others, she was a seamstress and sewed clothing and robes for others, she was well-loved by those around her based on their reaction when she died, she was possibly a widow based on vs. 41.

Q3. Answers may include: Jesus was showing how to serve others, even when you hold a higher place of status – teacher vs, disciple, an act of humility shows how humility is part of servanthood – which speaks to the heart. Disciples found this hard because they did not think they were worthy to have him wash their feet. He was their Rabbi!

Q4. Answers may include: Yes, because he was the older brother, he worked longer, he stayed with his father and didn't run off, he didn't squander his inheritance. Or, no, because he always had access to what his father had. It was selfishness because he felt he deserved the attention for his hard work, he wasn't grateful for what he had.

Q5. Answers may include: We are too busy, we don't know the people we should serve, they might be homeless and could be dangerous, it is too uncomfortable, it is not in my skill set to serve the way it is needed, it is inconvenient, it might turn to a long-term commitment I am not ready for or don't want.

Servanthood Alternative Learning Pages

<u>Activity 1</u> – Servanthood focuses on others; self-centeredness focuses on ourselves. Servanthood involves self-sacrifice of either time or money. It is sometimes inconvenient but is done anyway with a happy heart. Self-centeredness puts self-first above others, an unwillingness to set aside personal wants for the good of the other person. If it is inconvenient or requires too much of my time, I won't do it.

<u>Activity 2</u> –
- Tabitha - made garments and tunics for people; She served whoever needed them; She loved Jesus and people (inferred)

- Jesus- washed the disciples' feet; He served His disciples; To teach them how to serve

Activity 3 - words in order
Robes, Joppa, Peter, widows, Passover, washed, questioned, serve, Pharisees, righteous

Activity 4 –
1. Self-centeredness

Activity 5 –
1. She didn't really serve her mom because she served with a bad attitude.
2. Her reaction should have been to be willing and helpful even when she didn't feel like it.

Activity 6 –thoughtful, sacrifice, others, willing, kind, hard, give

Chapter 2 – Sexual Purity part 1

Q1. Answers will be inferred based on what we know of Joseph's character. However, no right or wrong answers. Possibilities include he exhibited integrity long before he was put in that situation. He knew God's law against sexual immorality so was taught those scriptures.

Q2. No – as with any choice we make to do the right thing, we always open ourselves up to be criticized, ridiculed or even physically harmed. It is important for us to surround ourselves with peers who are like-minded so we can support each other and encourage each other to stay true to our convictions even when it is hard. **PARENTS** – touch on the value of accountability, which is crucial in navigating the area of sexual purity.

Q3. Answers will vary based on child. **PARENTS** - Encourage them to set some personal purity goals as it relates to their bodies, modesty, physical contact with the opposite sex, boundaries. This can be a list or chart or even a contract they choose to sign.

Q4. Answers will vary but should include ideas of God's forgiveness. God forgets our sin and does not hold it against us. He is eager to forgive and shame has no place once we confess our sin. Joyful restoration awaits, God's grace is available to all of us.

Q5. Homosexuality verses (not an exhaustive list):
Genesis 19:1-13; Leviticus 18:22; Romans 1:26-27; 1 Corinthians 6:9-11; 1 Timothy 8:1-11

Q6. God's standard is for Christians to love others (not an exhaustive list):
Leviticus 19:18; Numbers 14:18; John 13:34; Romans 13:8; 1 Corinthians 13; Galatians 5:14; Colossians 3:12-14.

Q7. Answers will vary but should include: Christians should respond with love and compassion, not judgement and hate. God despises sexual sin, but he also despises lying, pride and hypocrisy. It is not our place to condemn but to draw people to experience the love of Jesus. We also are not to condone or give approval of a homosexual lifestyle. Separating the sin from the person means we can disagree with the choice, and not adhere to the ideology that "it's their truth so it is ok", but love the person, speak Biblical truth with grace and kindness when given the opportunity and pray for them.

Sexual Purity Alternative Learning Pages

Activity 1 - Answers may include: Joseph refuses to sleep with Potiphar's wife, he knew the boundary of not sleeping with another man's wife, he fled the temptation and did not stay in the situation.

Activity 2 - Answers may include: marriage is the foundation for building families, it is a representation of God and the church. Consequences: Children can be born outside of a marriage commitment, sex outside of marriage cheapens the act of sex, rather than seeing it as holy and set apart it is selfish and casual, regret, mistrust.

Activity 3 -
David's poor choices –
- he chose to stay home rather than go fight in battle as other Kings do
- he saw Bathsheba bathing and chose to stay and look
- he sent someone to go find out about her
- he told them to bring her to him
- had sex with her knowing she was married
- when she became pregnant, he had her husband killed

The better choice –
- he should have gone into battle with his men
- when he saw Bathsheba, he should have left the roof top
- he should have set his mind to other things and not Bathsheba
- upon finding out she was married he should have left it alone
- fleeing from the temptation

Activity 4 –
1. The child born to David and Bathsheba would die
2. He got up off the ground where he had been praying that his son would live, washed, put on clean clothes, and went to the temple to worship God. David recognized the seriousness of his sin and the all-powerful nature of God to discipline his children. David responded with humility rather than anger.
3. God continued to allow victory after victory in battle and protected David from his enemies. God kept his promise to David to keep his descendants on the throne.

Activity 5 –
- Possible ending for giving in to sexual sin: girl gets pregnant, loss of trust between parent and child, emotional scaring, guilt/shame, boy leaves girl alone to deal with consequences, girl manipulates boy to stay in relationship, rumors start, future relationships can be damaged, potential disease.

- Possible ending for fleeing temptation: boy and girl breakup if no sex, false accusations could be made if boy/girl is angry over break up, integrity is intact, parents can trust their child to make hard choices when faced with temptation, no guilt/shame, God has been honored, blessing received.

PARENTS: It's important to add to any discussion that a baby is a gift from God no matter how it enters the world. Choosing life over abortion is honoring to the Lord, even though it is a really hard decision to make. Also, lots of families lovingly accept an unwanted pregnancy and support and care for the young mother. It is not a death sentence and NOT anything that is unforgivable. God's blessing doesn't cease when mistakes are made. He redeems it all!

Chapter 3 - Discipline

Q1. He knew what was acceptable to eat as a Jew and what wasn't. He did not want to defile Himself and dishonor God by eating the food of the king. The king's food was likely attractive, smelled good and was very tasty. It took inner discipline to not even try it.

Q2. Answers may include: Daniel grew up with this knowledge and was likely taught from an early age to resist this type of food. He likely had already made the decision in his mind to not give in to the pressure to eat this type of food and did not have to make a quick in-the-moment decision.

Q3. Answers may include: anything worth doing well takes time, commitment and sometimes sacrifice and hard work. To be disciplined in something you often must give up something to have the reward at the end. It is often not easy because of what you must give up in order to attain it.

Q6. He does not work, things he has fall apart, takes no pride in work or what he has, poverty

Discipline Alternative Learning Pages

<u>Activity 2</u>
1. Courageous, determined, resolute, steadfast

Activity 5 – Crossword Puzzle Answers

Chapter 4 – Compassion

Q1. Answers may include: helping those in physical/emotional need; being willing to give financially to help someone else; understanding I don't need recognition when I show compassion.

Q2. Certain amount of his wages; possibly his reputation depending on who the stranger was (Jewish possibly.

Q3. They felt threatened by his growing popularity; they felt guilty for not showing compassion themselves.

Q5. Answers may include: we can be useful as either cold or hot but lukewarm serves no purpose

Q6. Answers may include: showing we do not care, we do not stand for anything, we are not willing to get our hands dirty and do the hard work of helping and making a difference, our words do not match our actions.

Compassion Alternative Learning Pages

Activity 1 – Answers may include: compassion is looking out for others' best interest, showing the love of Jesus to those who are hurting, sacrificing our own comforts to reach out to others, not ignoring the needs around us. Indifference is not caring for those around me who are hurting, not paying attention to the needs of the world, looking the other way because it is too much work.

Activity 2 -
- Good Samaritan – he stopped and helped because there was a need; a stranger, possibly an enemy; they were compelled, possibly out of a love of God

- Jesus – he healed on the sabbath; a man who had a shriveled hand; he was Jesus, and it is his nature; to teach a lesson.

Activity 3 -
1. The compassionate ending: options include his friends show up to defend him and no fight ensues; not only do friends show up but a mob of students show up to support Danny and Joseph runs away; Danny talks Joseph down. Any other positive compassionate response.
2. The indifferent ending: options include others watch Joseph pick on Danny, but no one does anything
3. The compassionate ending honors God. It is not always easy to show compassion because you may be picked on next.

Activity 5 -
- Compassion words – honoring God, sacrificing your time for others, heart breaks for the hurting, helping when it is inconvenient.

- Indifference words – ignoring needs around you, it does not affect me why should I help, walking on by, you do not have time to help.

Chapter 5 – Integrity

Q1. She was the second wife, having no children while wife #1 did, wife #1 would mock her, year after year, even during worship at the temple, she had a husband that did not understand her grief, Priest Eli thought she was drunk when she was praying at the temple.

Q2. She continued to go to the temple to worship and pray, made a vow to God, she believed what Eli spoke to her and had confidence in God's promise.

Q3. She fulfilled her vow, promising God that if he gave her a son, she would present him to the Lord and have him live in the temple and serve God. Likely not an easy decision as she was giving up her son at a young age and may have only gotten to see him once a year when she went up to the temple.

Q4. He was greedy (covetous), he kept some of the plunder for himself, he likely did not think he would get caught.

Q6. Answers may include: not being able to keep a job, or get one if you have a bad reputation, not having the trust of family or friends because you have lied too many times or been untrustworthy, lack of true friendship, a distant relationship with God because he does not bless the dishonorable. It matters so others can depend on us.

Integrity Alternative Learning Pages

Activity 1 – Integrity answers could include a strong moral compass, honest, a character that is the same in private as in public. Dishonor answers could include dishonest, not trustworthy.

Activity 2 - Answers may include: honesty, obedience, dependable, punctual, purity

Activity 3 – Answers may include: anger at God, bitterness against the other wife, revenge and anger against husband. God may not have blessed her with Samuel. And even if she did have Samuel, she may not have kept her promise to God and given him to the temple. Samuel may not have become a priest which would have had lasting ramifications on all the lives Samuel touched in his life as a prophet.

Activity 4 –
- Words for Achan:
  Bar of Gold; devoted things; God's anger burned; silver; stoning; destruction; treasury

- Words for Hannah:
  devotion; weeping; temple; priest; rival; offering; Given over to the Lord

Chapter 6 – Courage

Q1. Whether or not to confront the king about the edict to kill the Jews.

Q2. Answers may include: being put in prison, banishment, being killed, her whole household could be killed.

Q6. Answers may include: because we are choosing to trust Him to be with us, it grows our faith, shows we depend on Him. It is important because fear is doubting God's ability to help us.

Courage Alternative Learning Pages

Activity 1 – Esther 5-9 Details may include: She was a Jewish girl. The king was looking for a new queen, so all young women were brought to the palace and put through rigorous cleansing, beauty treatments, etc. to prepare to meet the king. Esther was chosen. She discovered a plot by Haman to kill all the Jew's. Mordecai, her relative, told her that her purpose in being queen was to talk to the king and inform him of the evil plot. She was put there for a reason. This was risky because if you approached the king without being invited you could be killed. Her life hung in the balance. She implored her people to pray for her and after several days she showed incredible courage and approached the king. He was pleased to have her enter his presence and desired to honor her requests. She told the truth about Haman and as a result the king had him killed and the Jews were spared.

Activity 5 – Answers could include: Peter could have been killed along with Jesus. At the least he could have had his reputation ruined and been persecuted.

Activity 7 – Word Search Answers

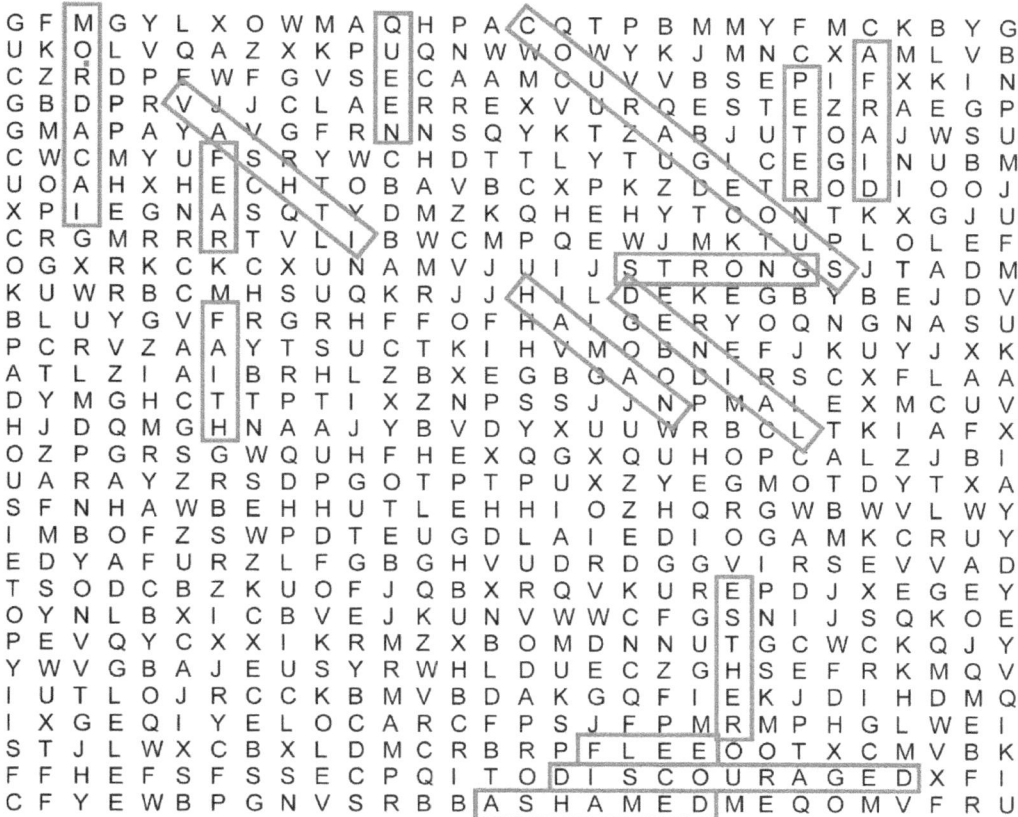

Chapter 7 – Self-Control

Q1. Answers for self-controlled actions: emotional restraint, obedience, honor, respect versus self-indulgent actions: fleshly desire, greed, knowledge above God.

Answers for summary: Self-control requires the ability to put self aside and focus on the end goal, delayed gratification and what honors the Lord in that moment. Self-Indulgence is selfish. It does not think about the consequences and leaves God and his holiness out of the picture.

Q2.
a. These men prayed to God for wisdom and protection when confronted with a difficult situation.
b. He likely prayed for strength to thrive during those 10 days so to find favor with the king.

Q3. Prayer is important as it shows our need to rely on God, expresses our desire to honor him with our choices and gives us the strength to stand firm in our convictions.

Q5. Answers may include:
- self-control requires restraint for something we want immediately. Harder to put off than to have now.

- Nehemiah answer: dragging the Jews into a battle, the heavy loss of life

- an unfinished wall susceptible to foreign enemies.

Q6. Answers may include
- Possible blessings: respect, dependable, fewer regrets for speaking or acting impulsively

- Benefit of "wall": protection from intruders, keep safe that which is inside

Self-Control Alternative Learning Pages

Activity 2 –
- Self-controlled actions include: not retaliating, staying the course, not seeking revenge, refraining from eating delicious food

- Self-indulgent actions include: giving up a sacred secret, desiring to be like God and satisfy a fleshly desire, giving in to sinful sexual pleasure

Activity 6 – Words in order:
David, gratification, not cutting his hair, prayed, Adam and Eve, restraint, fleshly, rebuild, vegetables, king's food, work, spear

Chapter 8 – Humility

Q1. Answers may include: unforgiveness, arrogance, false humility, impatience with God, failure to admit mistakes, thinking only of self

Q3. Answers may include: he reminded himself of his purpose, worshiped who he knew to be the Messiah, corrected his followers when they were tempted to praise him, used thankfulness as a tool for humility

Q5. Answers may include: he justified his actions, used the excuse of needing God's favor, did not seek repentance and forgiveness, he did not humble himself.

Humility Alternative Learning Pages

Activity 1 –
- Possible words for humble – repentance, does not talk about themselves, asks questions of others, quick to apologize, seeks to understand

- Possible words for pride – thinks of themselves, does not seem interested in others, does not apologize when wrong, likes to talk about themselves

Activity 4 – Answers will vary but may include:
1. With thankfulness/gratefulness, acknowledge our talents come from the Lord
2. It will get hard and grow cold to where are talents truly come from, we will be brought low (humbled by God)

Activity 5
- Pride Words:
  excuses, impatience, arrogance, King Saul, independence, Pride of Life, strife, always right

- Humility Words:
  John the Baptist, repentance, dependence, advice, others first, worship, expectant faith, teachable

Activity 7 – Words in Order:
worthy, waiting, rich, animal, praised, honored, glorified, humbled, guides, teaches, pride, arrogance, lust, lust, pride, Father, world

Chapter 9 - Obedience

Q1. Answers may include: asking some legitimate questions, allowing it to be so, submitting to the will of God, feeling unworthy, questioning the truth of what's being said, "but how did she get pregnant?"

Q2. Mary asked how this could be true while she was still a virgin. She also said, "I am the Lord's servant. May your word to me be fulfilled." This played out in the song she sings in her heart to the Lord, she submits to the will of God. Jospeh also submits to the will of God and changes his mind to divorce her. He was likely quite worried about how this would turn out.

Q3. Answers will vary based on version chosen. Some versions may include NIV, MSG, NLT, NKJV. Google Bible Translations for a more complete list.

Q4. Answers may include various viewpoints:
- unwarranted since he was always obedient except for this one time, he was faithful in delivering God's punishment to the Israelites and scolded them for their disobedience

- warranted since he disobeyed, he mislead the Israelites in his disobedience, he was the leader and did not do as he was told, he was held to a greater level of accountability, God needed to make Moses an example to the Israelites to show the importance of obeying God

Obedience Alternative Learning Pages

Activity 1 - Answers may include:
obedience verses mention twice that long life is the result, disobedience verses mention twice curses from God or hand of God against the disobedient

Activity 2 - Answers include:
- Obedient - willingness to follow God in the unknown, a resolution to obey without all the answers – result – blessing, help along the way

- Disobedient – fear/cowardice - consequences – not entering Canaan, being thrown into sea, eaten by a fish, guilt of running from God.

Activity 6 – Words in order:
struck, rock, followed, Highly Favored, word, fulfilled, blessed, honor, Israelite

Chapter 10 – Wisdom

Q1. Answers may include: more wealth, foreign nations to submit to him, conquer more land, win all their battles. He saw the value of having wisdom as a king given all the decisions he would be required to make. It shows he wanted to honor God as he ruled

Q2. Answers may include: he recognized his surroundings and the potential dangers of a soft foundation; he was able to look to the future and what types of weather could impact the stability of his home. The outcome is that his house stood firm when the weather hit. He was not affected by the weather. He could rest assured that he'd be safe

Q3. Answers may include: he did not trust God for his protection, so he bribed another nation to attack his enemy, causing that country to break a treaty. His consequence was that he was at war instead of at peace, he oppressed his people, even in physical affliction he refused to repent of his foolishness

Q4. Answers may include: they wanted something to worship and got tired of waiting for Moses. It was a foolish decision because they didn't trust God, they made an impulsive decision in their impatience.

Q7.
a. Multiple possible answers but could include: college choice, getting married, parenting questions, job choices, moving, how to spend money/investing
b. Potential outcomes for foolish choices: marrying the wrong person (out of God's will), hurting children by making wrong parenting choices, taking the wrong job and being miserable, losing a lot of money by investing/spending unwisely
c. Importance of wise choices now – training for future, practice seeking God now, so we seek God later for more important decisions

Wisdom Alternative Learning Pages

Activity 1
1. wisdom and understanding
2. words of insight
3. instruction in prudent behavior
4. doing what is right and just and fair
5. giving prudence to those who are simple
6. knowledge and discretion to the young

Activity 2 – Answers may include: he assessed his situation, and his foundation and determined the best type of home to permanently last would be built on rocks. He applied knowledge and understanding to his situation.

Activity 4 – Word search answers

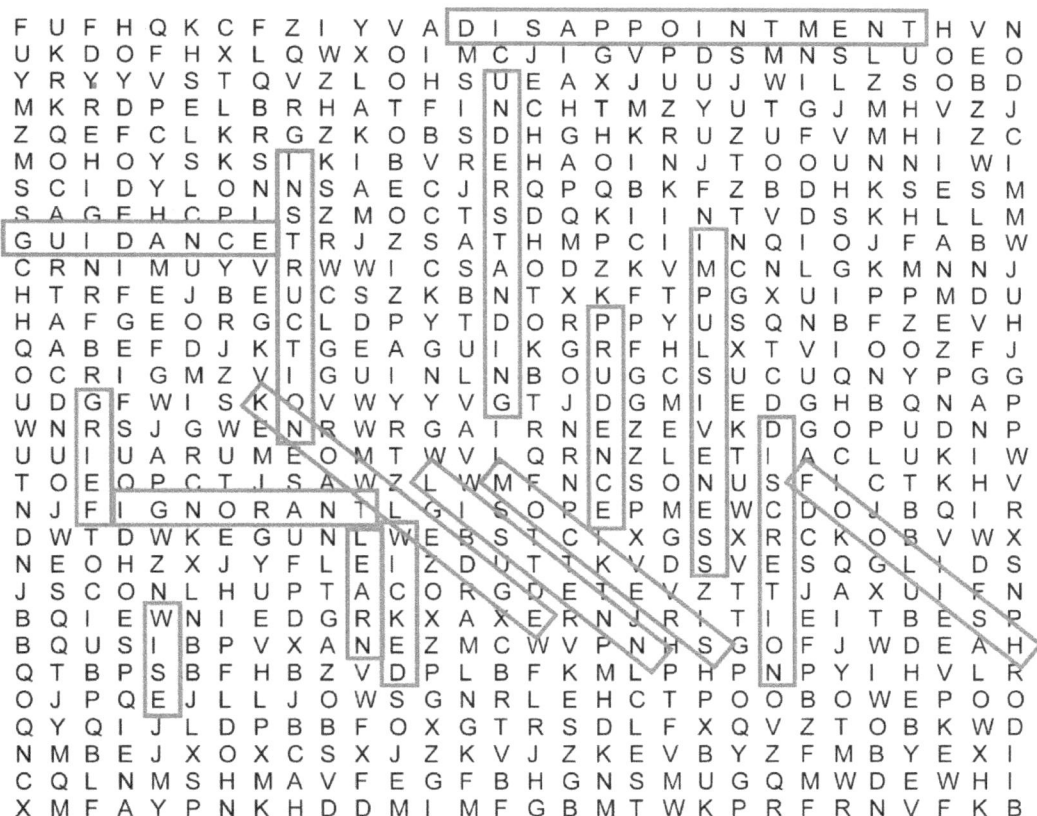

Chapter 11 – Forgiveness

Q2 – Answers may include: the Father loved his son unconditionally so forgiving him was not an option. The Father saw the humility and contrite attitude of the son. He saw an understanding of the wrong he had done and the burden of the consequences. He had compassion on him. Was it easy? Maybe yes and no based on the process the father went through in the son's absence to come to terms with the hurtful choices of his on.

Q4. Answers may include: forgiveness is not a condition of salvation, but it is a requirement for believers. Unforgiveness is an ungodly act and our sins we commit as Christians will not be forgiven by God if we willingly withhold forgiveness from others. When we confess our sin of unforgiveness He will forgive us absolutely.

Q5. Answers may include: Joseph recognized that God had a purpose for him which included a location change to Egypt. Joseph knew that God's purpose was good and would use the evil done to him to fulfill that purpose. The result of his forgiveness was being reconciled to his brothers and joyful reunion. His gracious compassion and forgiveness softened their hearts and brought about repentance. Possibly, if Joseph was not forgiving, God would not have blessed his leadership in Egypt, his brothers would not have reconciled, they would not have moved their families to Egypt and the Israel nation would not have experienced the blessings of God.

Forgiveness Alternative Learning Pages

Activity 1 –
1. Thrown into a pit
2. Sold as a slave
3. Falsely Accused of rape
4. Put in prison
5. Helped fellow prisoners
6. They failed to vouch for him when they were released

Activity 2 – Possible answer included him recognizing God had a plan for his life and would use the tragic things done to him to bring about a greater purpose.

Activity 4 – Crossword Puzzle answers –

```
                            R           D
                  G R I E V A N C E
          F     P         P           C
    C A I N     R         E           E
          R     O F F E N S E         I
          S     D         T     F A V O R
          T     I         E           E
    J   F O R G I V E N E S S         D
    A     R     A         S   L
    C     U     L         E   A       J
    O     I                   V       O
    B I T T E R N E S S       E       S
          S     O         G R A C E
                O             Y       P
                T                     H
```

Citations

1. Mother Teresa Quote. (n.d.). Lib Quotes. https://libquotes.com/mother-teresa/quote/lbv2v9x.

2. Jamison, H., Reclaiming Intimacy: Overcoming the Consequences of Premarital Relationships, (Kregel Publications, 2001), 29.

3. Dictionary.com, (2018), http://www.dictionary.com.

4. Laziness Quotes (350 quotes). (n.d.). https://www.goodreads.com/quotes/tag/laziness?page=3 – Benjamin Franklin.

5. Dictionary.com, (2018), http://www.dictionary.com.

6. Passiton.com, https://www.passiton.com/inspirational-quotes/7300-courage-doesnt-always-roar-sometimes-courage - Mary Anne Radmacher.

7. Billy Graham Quotes, (n.d.). BrainyQuote, https://www.brainyquote.com/quotes/billy_graham_1136227.

8. Got Self-Control? (2016, October 21), Focus on the Family, https://www.focusonthefamily.com/parenting/got-self-control/- Ted Cunningham.

9. David Wilkerson, The Awful Sin of Pride, February 8, 1988. (n.d.), http://www.tscpulpitseries.org/english/1980s/ts880208.html.

10. Ibid.

11. Pride and Humility, C.S. Lewis Institute. (n.d.), https://www.cslewisinstitute.org/Pride_and_Humility_SinglePage.

12. Tomlin, C. (2010), I Will Follow [Review of I Will Follow]. Dan Muckala, You Tube Link: Chris Tomlin - I Will Follow [With Lyrics]. (n.d.). https://www.youtube.com/watch?v=g02mOpdNDtY.

13. Dictionary.com, (2018), http://www.dictionary.com.

14. The Pursuit of Holiness, Quotes by Jerry Bridges, (n.d.). https://www.goodreads.com/work/quotes/252777-the-pursuit-of-holiness.

15. Keller, T., & Keller, K., God's Wisdom for Navigating Life: A Year of Daily Devotions in the Book of Proverbs, (Viking, 2017) 28.

16. Keller, T. & Keller. K., God's Wisdom for Navigating Life, 7.

17. Luther, M., Warnock, R. G., & Coretta Scott King, A Gift of Love: Sermons from Strength to Love and Other Preachings, (Penguin, 2017).

18. Sauls, S., A Gentle Answer: Our "Secret Weapon" in an Age of Us Against Them, (Nelson Books, 2020), 146.

19. West, M. (2012). Forgiveness [Review of Forgiveness], Peter Kipley. Matthew West - Forgiveness (Official Lyric Video) - Music Video [YouTube Video]. In YouTube. https://www.youtube.com/watch?v=FMn0QNdiuGE

www.ingramcontent.com/pod-product-compliance
Lightning Source LLC
Chambersburg PA
CBHW081741100526
44592CB00015B/2249